JAKUB
JULIAN
ZIÓŁKOWSKI

ΔΕΣΤΕ

DESTE Foundation for Contemporary Art

JAKUB JULIAN ZIÓŁKOWSKI

2000 WORDS

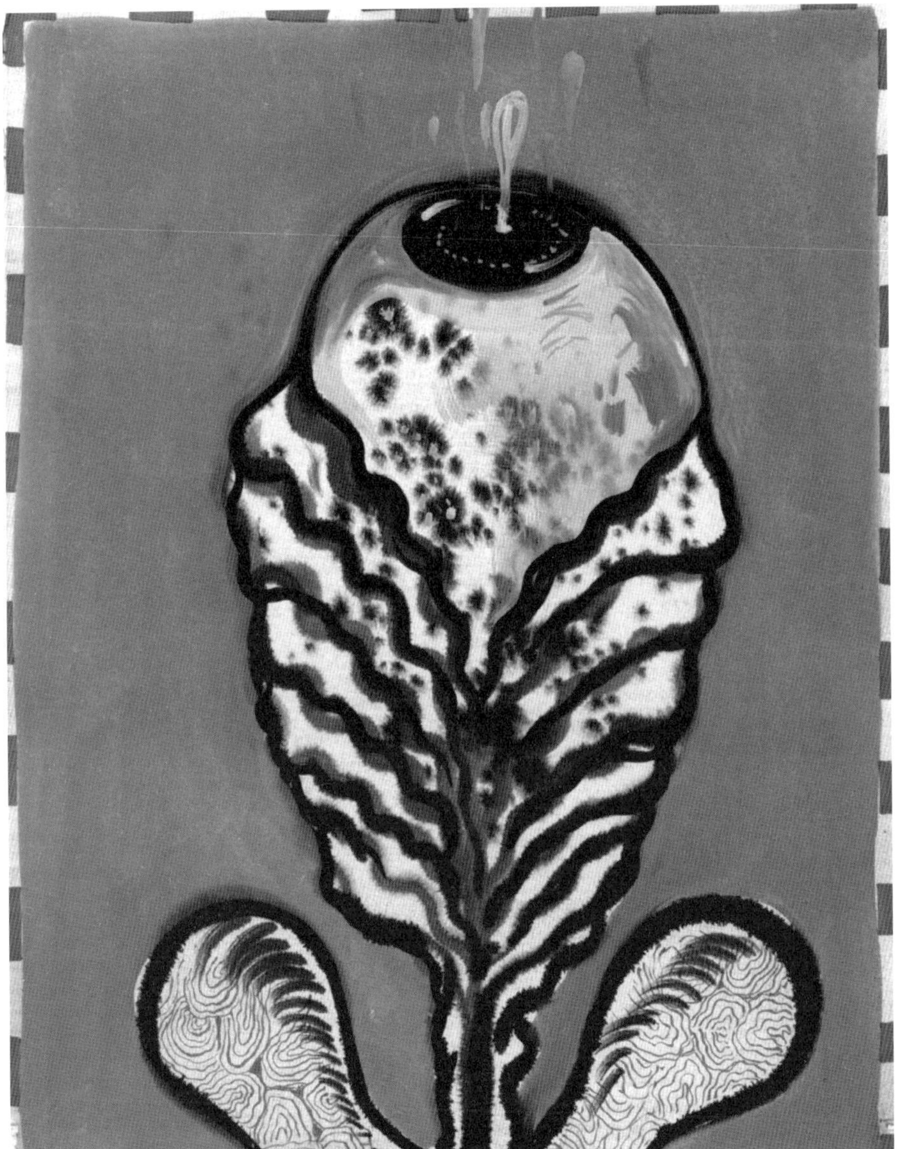

THE SOLAR ANUS

Cecilia Alemani

The first time I visited Jakub Julian Ziółkowski in his studio in Krakow, Poland, he told me about a self-taught Polish painter named Nikifor, who was a very pious, religious man until the day he took a trip on an airplane and, up there among the clouds, realized there was no God. A similar tension between spirituality and blasphemy pervades the work of Jakub Julian Ziółkowski. The universes conjured by his paintings collapse onto each other heavenly visions and debased primordial needs; in his work the innocent and the perverse live side by side.

Born in 1980, Ziółkowski grew up in Zamość, a small town sixty kilometers from the Polish border with Ukraine that has been historically considered an extraordinary example of utopian urban planning. Designed in 1580 by the Italian architect Bernardo Morando, Zamość was planned as a settlement that would combine an innovative approach to urban design with the Renaissance model of the ideal city, aspiring to become a gathering place for people from different cultures, nations, and religions. Unlike many cities in Poland, which were destroyed during World War II and completely rebuilt in its aftermath, Zamość still stands today as a remarkable example of Polish Renaissance architecture with its celebration of the arts and its belief in the secret correspondences between the micro- and the macrocosms, between man and the universe.

Perhaps it would be a stretch to argue that Ziółkowski's paintings, with their intricate systems of bewildered sympathies between the realms of the microscopic and the celestial, have been inspired by some distant Renaissance belief in the magic symmetry of the universe or by Zamość itself. But it probably wouldn't be too far-fetched to observe that in Ziółkowski's world one can detect the survival of a faith in the power of the mysterious affinities which link together different substances and creatures, disparate materials and forms—the human and the supernatural.

And if such a faith cannot be entirely traced back to the solar cosmologies of the Renaissance, it can certainly be linked to their darker counterparts. After all, the Renaissance dream of order also feeds the ebullient chaos of Hieronymus Bosch and the Pantagruelic appetite of François Rabelais. Throughout the 15th and 16th centuries, under the apparent clarity of humanist thought, much murkier waters continued to bubble, cooking up a potion in which medieval traditions and popular beliefs were combined to produce what art historians have called an "anti-renaissance" or a "dark renaissance."[1]

It is in this muddy underworld that Ziółkowski's work has put down roots. His iconography, with its abundance of mutant plants and fetid vegetation, could be grafted onto that incredibly intricate family tree which connects the darker side of 16th-century art—for the sake of brevity, let's say Bosch and Matthias Grűnewald—with the hallucinations of Le Douanier Henri Rousseau and the epiphanies of Max Ernst, all the way up to the mutilated figures of Philip Guston or the tumescent ones of Peter Saul. And it doesn't really matter that Ziółkowski might not even be fully aware of being part of such a noble and putrid lineage: like many of the prophets of this debased aesthetic, Ziółkowski seems to—or pretends to—operate in a perennial present in which different strands of art history coexist in a raucous cacophony of forms.

History itself has been a subject that Ziółkowski has tackled in many of his paintings, often with the enthusiasm of a Don Quixote and the vehemence of a fool. Crucifixions and war scenes are among his favorite scenarios; he takes on subjects and themes tinted by delusions of grandeur. In his work, in fact, Ziółkowski seems to interpret the role of a self-taught, naïf artist agitated by paranoid thoughts and illusions. It's difficult to say whether this self-stylization as an eccentric is to be interpreted as a conscious tactic or if he actually identifies and sympathizes with that kind of sensibility. Ziółkowski is a trained painter who has studied art history, but his work seems to reveal a predilection for minor traditions and obscure references, for an outsider-ish streak. Perhaps trying to distinguish sincerity from affectation is not even that relevant here, for it is precisely the coexistence of these opposing tensions that gives Ziółkowski's work its peculiar intensity. More importantly, Ziółkowski's work first of all urges us to look, to stare and focus: it is an adventure for the eyes—even an infection of the eyes—and as such it engages with minutiae and with the minor.

Take for instance *The Great Battle Under the Table* (2006), one of the paintings that brought Ziółkowski to international attention when it was included in the New Museum's 2009 Triennial, *Younger Than Jesus*. This dense canvas depicts a battle scene that takes place underneath a modest table, which occupies the center of the composition. On the floor beneath it, hundreds of small creatures—tiny little men wearing red and blue uniforms, comparatively gigantic animals making their way through the landscape, and disproportioned objects that seem to have been magically animated—crawl in a disorderly manner, covering the entire surface of the floor. Like little toy soldiers brought to life, the combatants move without clear strategy or order, perhaps following the guidance of what appears to be Napoleon, a towering figure standing at the top of an unrealistically large chair. All over the ground, diminutive landscapes open up like miniaturized Flemish paintings, bustling with activity like a swarming beehive: gentle hills are suddenly occupied by an army of cannons, a Tower of Babel–like structure is turned into an infernal battlefield, and several flowerpots are made into bunkers by the mini-militia and by colossal skeletons. While this world unravels under the table, another scene animates its upper surface: succulent plants, hats, masks, and everyday objects fill the yellow tabletop. A number of little men take possession of this peaceful still life, turning it into another battlefield where plants are used as trampolines to launch parachutists to the battle below and a bottle of water is flipped to the side, its liquid transformed into an improvised weapon against the army underneath. One could only try in vain to describe such an intricate painting, for it combines a meticulous, even maniacal, attention to detail with the vast breadth of a historical narrative, in which men and nature are entangled in a never-ending battle. Like many of his other works, this painting is almost a living, self-germinating organism, in which some of Ziółkowski's recurring obsessions with death, violence, sex, and religion are at the same time glorified and vilified, ridiculed and celebrated. Ziółkowski's carnivalesque universe refuses hierarchies, and offers instead an ever more slippery territory in which categories are constantly questioned.

Nowhere is this attitude more apparent than in Ziółkowski's portraiture. With his peculiar form of grotesque realism, Ziółkowski has composed a vast gallery of imaginary characters whose faces and bodies appear to be deformed by constant shifts in scale and by unexpected combinations of incongruous forms and organs. His delirious vivisections of the human body are based on a hallucinatory anatomy in which limbs can replace eyes, intestines colonize oral cavities, and genitals turn into bulbous digestive systems: any rigid categorization is refused, while condensation appears to be the reigning principle of Ziółkowski's biology.

The fact that Ziółkowski is the son of two doctors, and his father is an urologist, adds a surge of biographical evidence to his phantasmagoria of disembodied body parts. Ziółkowski grew up looking at anatomical models and medical illustrations, and hearing his parents speak about operations and emergency room adventures. And yet his bodies remain rebellious to order, impermeable to any logic. They are against authority and austerity: gluttonous and excessive, open and penetrative, polymorphous and singular—less bodies without organs than organs without bodies.

It is in the series of 69 gouaches inspired by Georges Bataille's renowned novel *Story of the Eye* that Jakub Julian Ziółkowski gives free reign to his anatomical fantasies, resulting in one of his most ambitious and disturbing works to date. Originally published in 1928 under the pseudonym of Lord Auch to protect Bataille from the inevitable backlash against its incendiary content, the novel tells the story of two teenage lovers who explore their sexuality through a series of vignettes embedded with erotic perversions, exhibitionist lusts, and orgiastic adventures. But what lurks beneath these tales is a much more complicated narrative, almost a subversive cosmology, in which the eye—the real protagonist of the novel—emerges as a metaphor for human desire and for a new epistemology, a new system of knowledge, and a whole new territory of experience.

As Roland Barthes put it,[2] Bataille describes the adventures of the eye through various cycles of avatars: the round shape of the ocular bulb is evoked by, and transformed through, a chain of metamorphoses into a series of other images and forms. The story follows two distinct metaphorical journeys, which are intertwined and alternate throughout the novel: that of the form of the eye, which is mirrored in a series of other images, such as that of a dish of milk, an egg, and a testicle; and that of the content of the eye, which, as the novel proceeds, turns from tears into milk, egg yolk, sperm, and urine. Bataille removes the eye from its traditional, idealistic valuations, which define it as a symbol of beauty or as a privileged means of knowledge, and instead degrades it to a base, material object, which is dirtied, mutilated, defaced, pretty much as it would happen in the famous scene of the eye castration in Luis Buñuel's *Un Chien Andalou*, which was presented one year after Bataille's novel appeared in France.

As Barthes observes, *Story of the Eye* is a machine for destroying hierarchies. Bataille has written a novel that refuses to privilege any of the images that recur throughout its pages: as the eye turns into the egg, which turns into a testicle, the novel drifts sideways. It is not a "deep work," writes Barthes; "everything in it is on the surface; there is no hierarchy." As a result, "the world becomes blurred," washed out, as Bataille writes, under the "urinary liquefaction of the sky." With this continuous ricocheting of forms, Bataille proceeds to demolish "the usual contiguities of objects," attaining a "general contagion of qualities and actions."

In his *Story of the Eye* (2010), Ziółkowski reaches a similar effect: every organ in the series appears to be contaminated, its confines violated, subjugated to some viral diffusion which spreads from body to body, annihilating differences and creating new, unexpected sympathies across substances and surfaces. Just as though they were infected by some kind of mysterious disease, the same images and forms seem to migrate from drawing to drawing, reproducing themselves as neoplasms: the spherical shape of the eye spreading into a variety of contexts and subjects, returning always identical and always different, first as a genital organ, then as some kind of tumor, as feces, as secretion. It is this blurring of the world, this transgression of values and definitions that Barthes sees as the avowed principle of eroticism: a counter-division which makes Ziółkowski's work so erotic, slippery, and complex. A contagious, mucous wetness seems to dampen the gouaches in this series. Ziółkowski, like Bataille before him, searches the interiors of his bodies like a haruspex, looking for signs of a new order of things: a nonhierarchical image of the universe.

1 See Roberto Longhi and his concept of *rinascimento umbratile* in *Edizione delle opere complete di Roberto Longhi*, 14 vols. (Florence: Sansoni, 1956–1991), and Eugenio Battisti's notion of *antirinascimento* in *L'Antirinascimento* (Milan: Nino Aragno, 1962).

2 Roland Barthes, "Hommage à Georges Bataille," in *Critique*, nos. 195–6, August–September 1963.

WORKS

Untitled, 2008

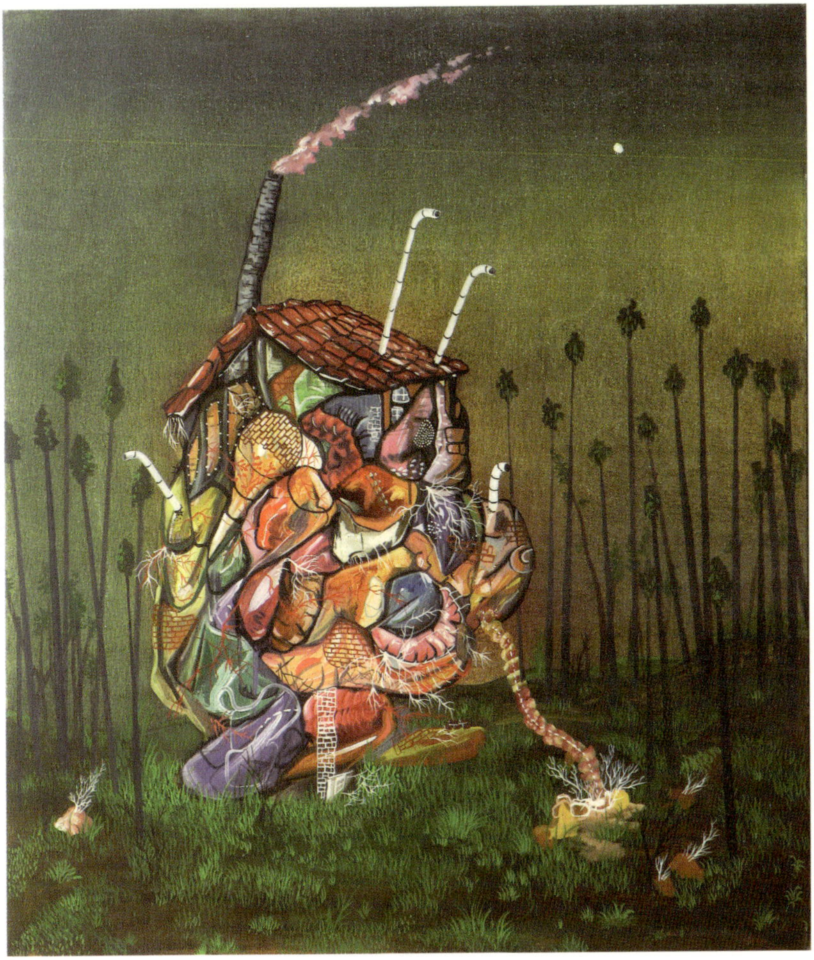

Untitled (Bobby), 2008

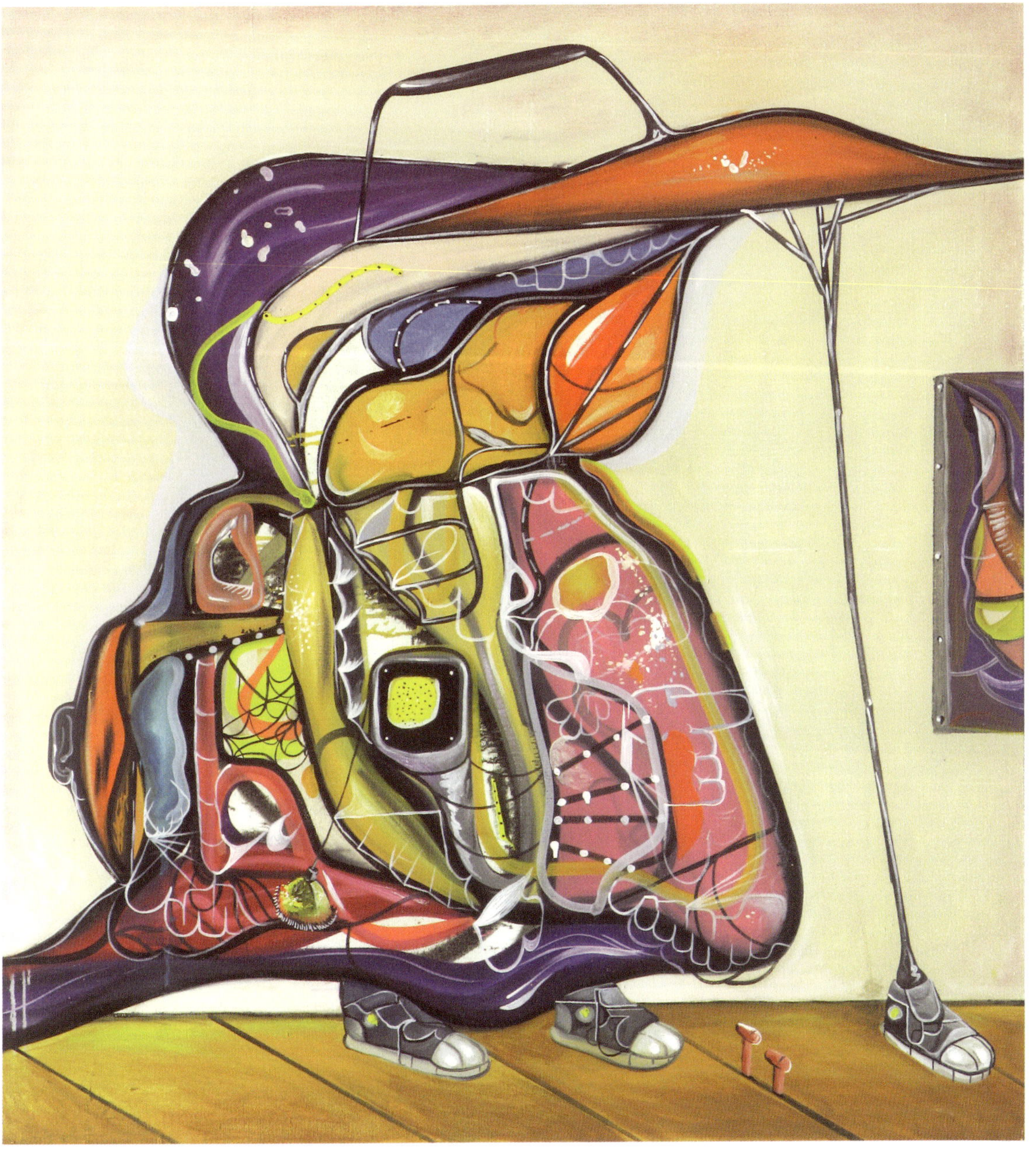

Untitled, 2009

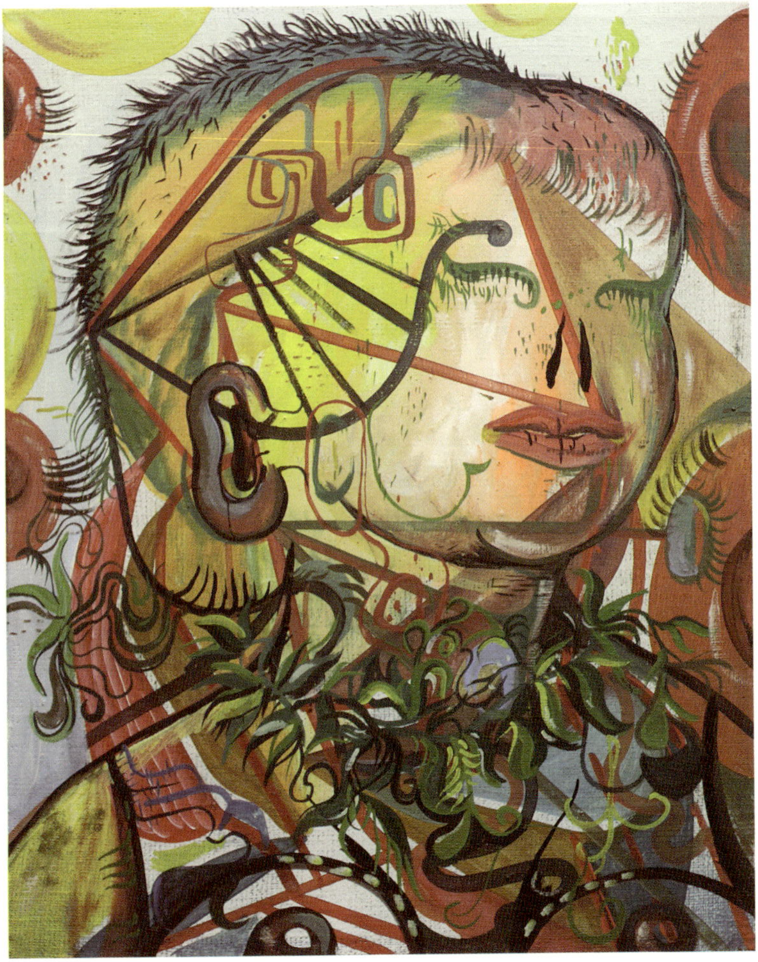

Untitled, 2009

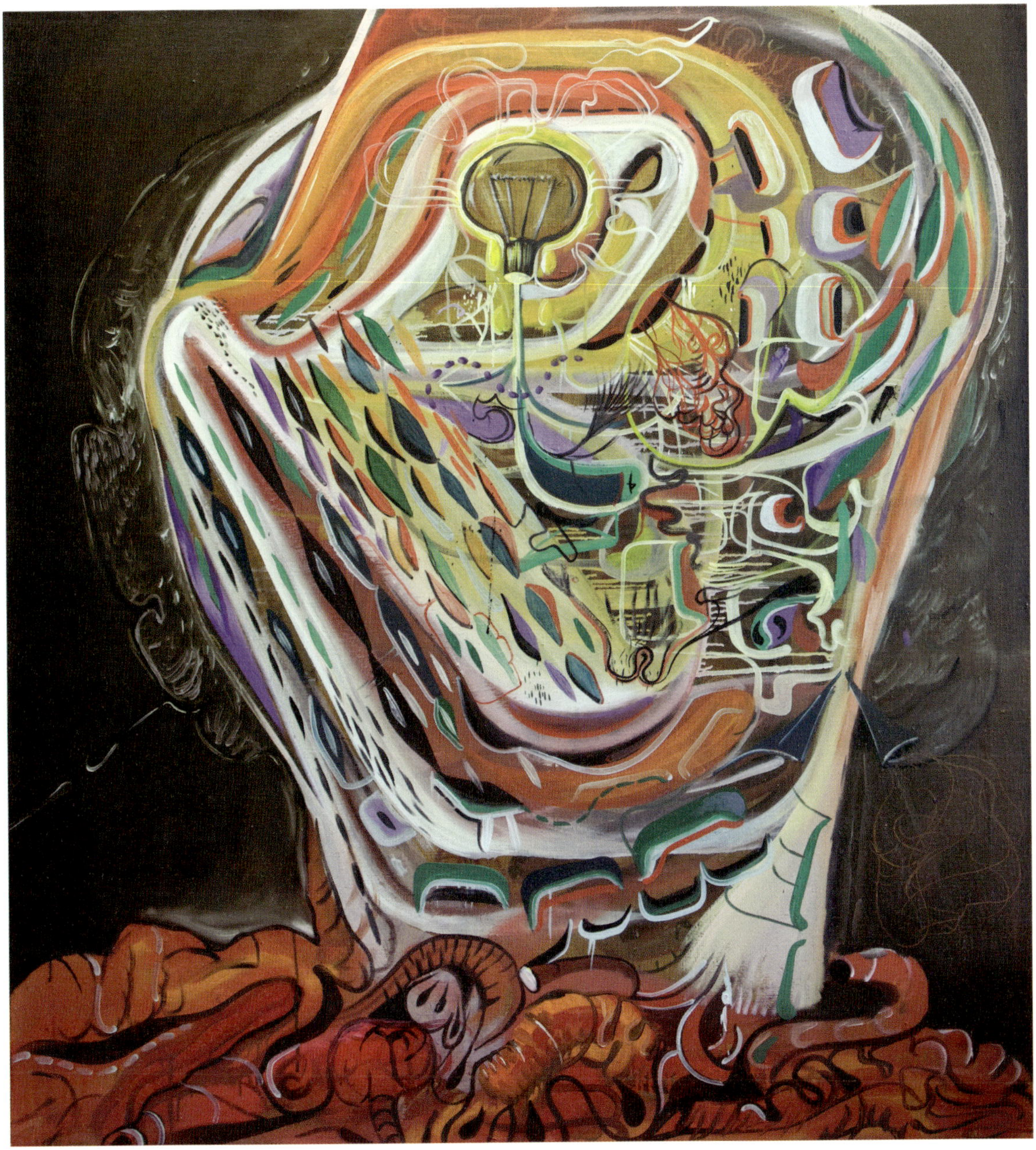

Untitled, 2009

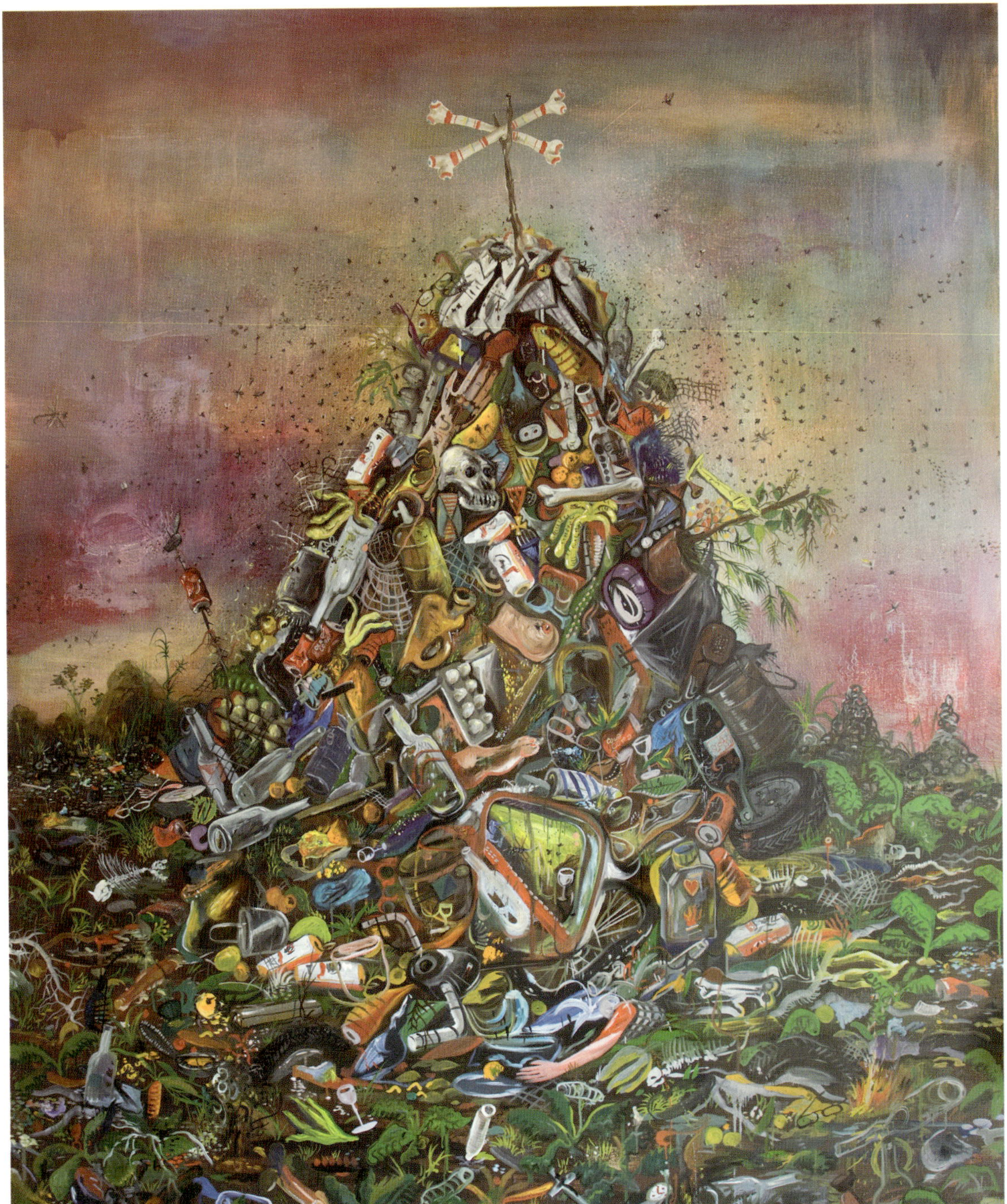

Monk, 2009

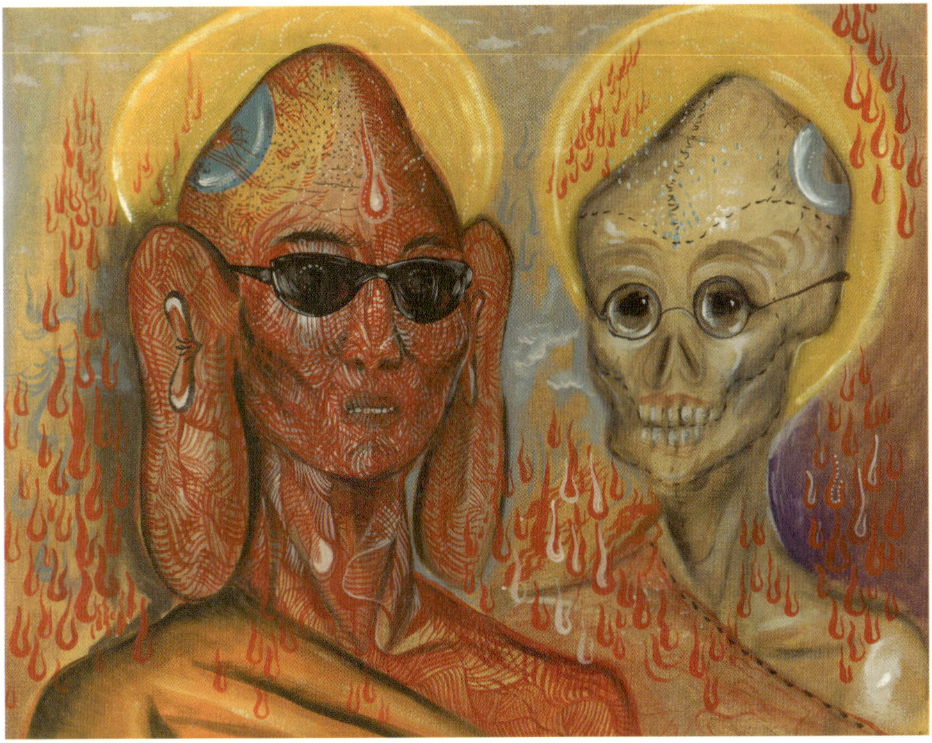

Untitled, 2010

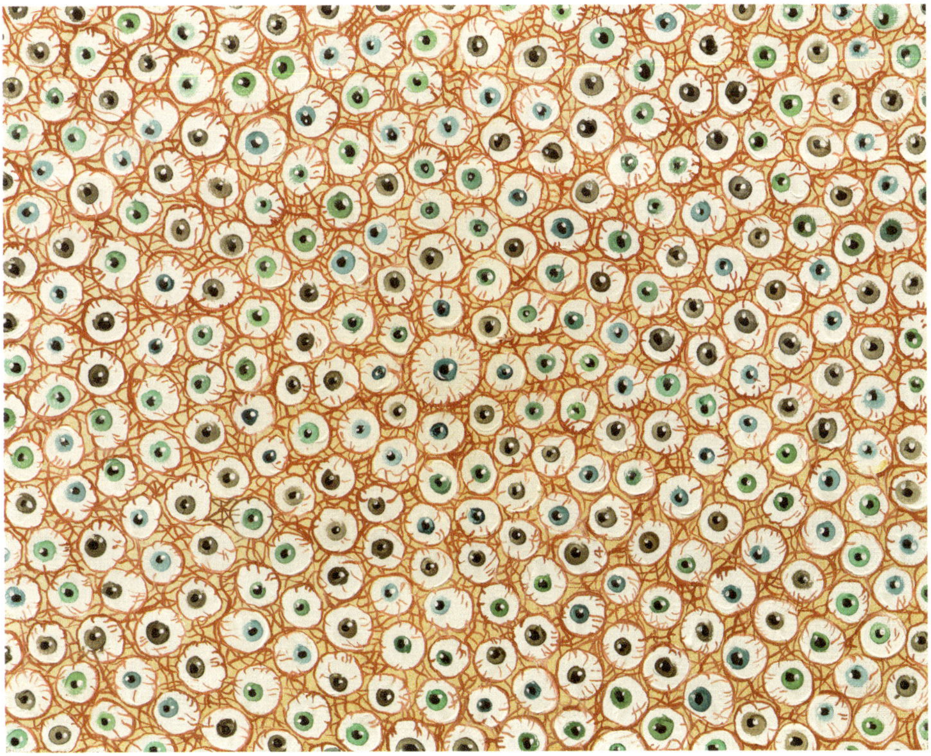

Untitled (King of Israel), 2010

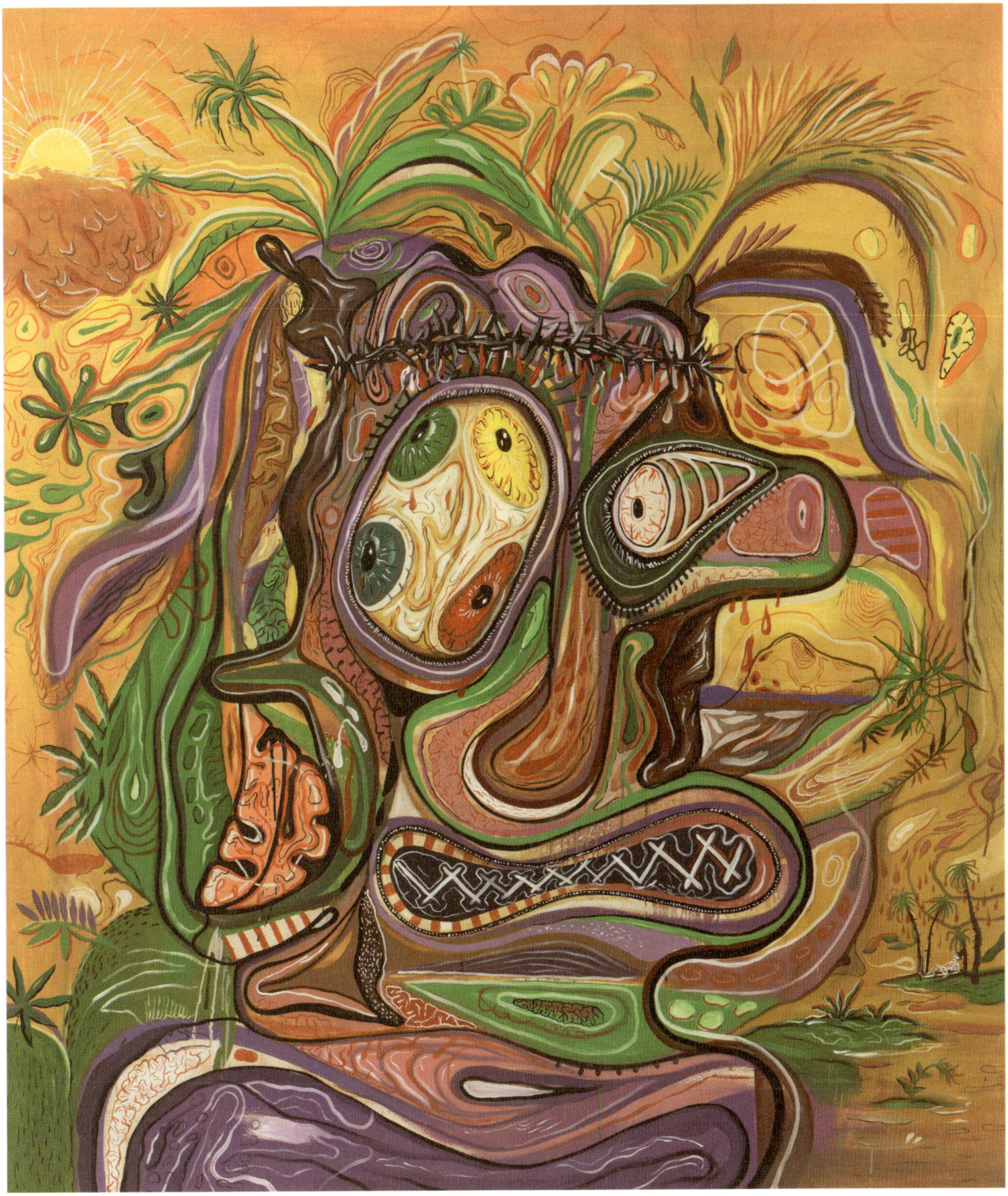

Skin and Bread, 2011

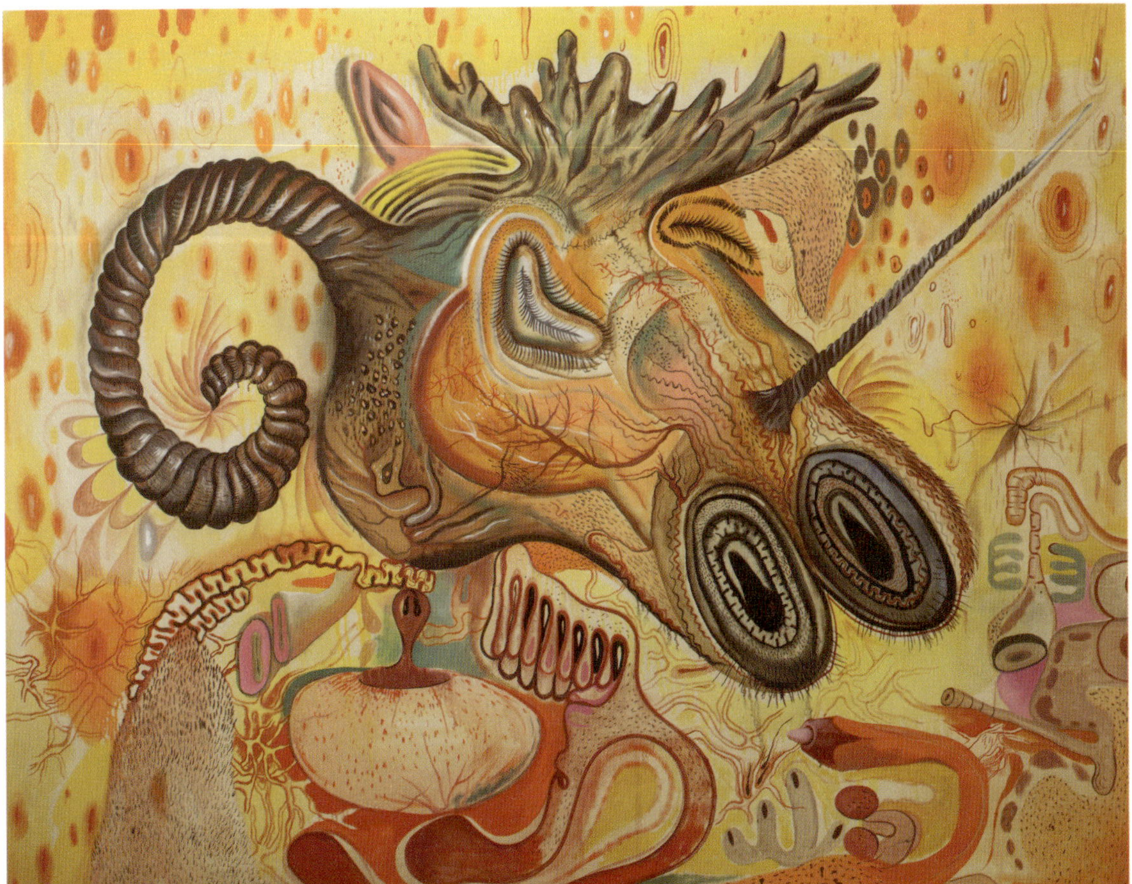

The Blood (The Holy Blood), 2011

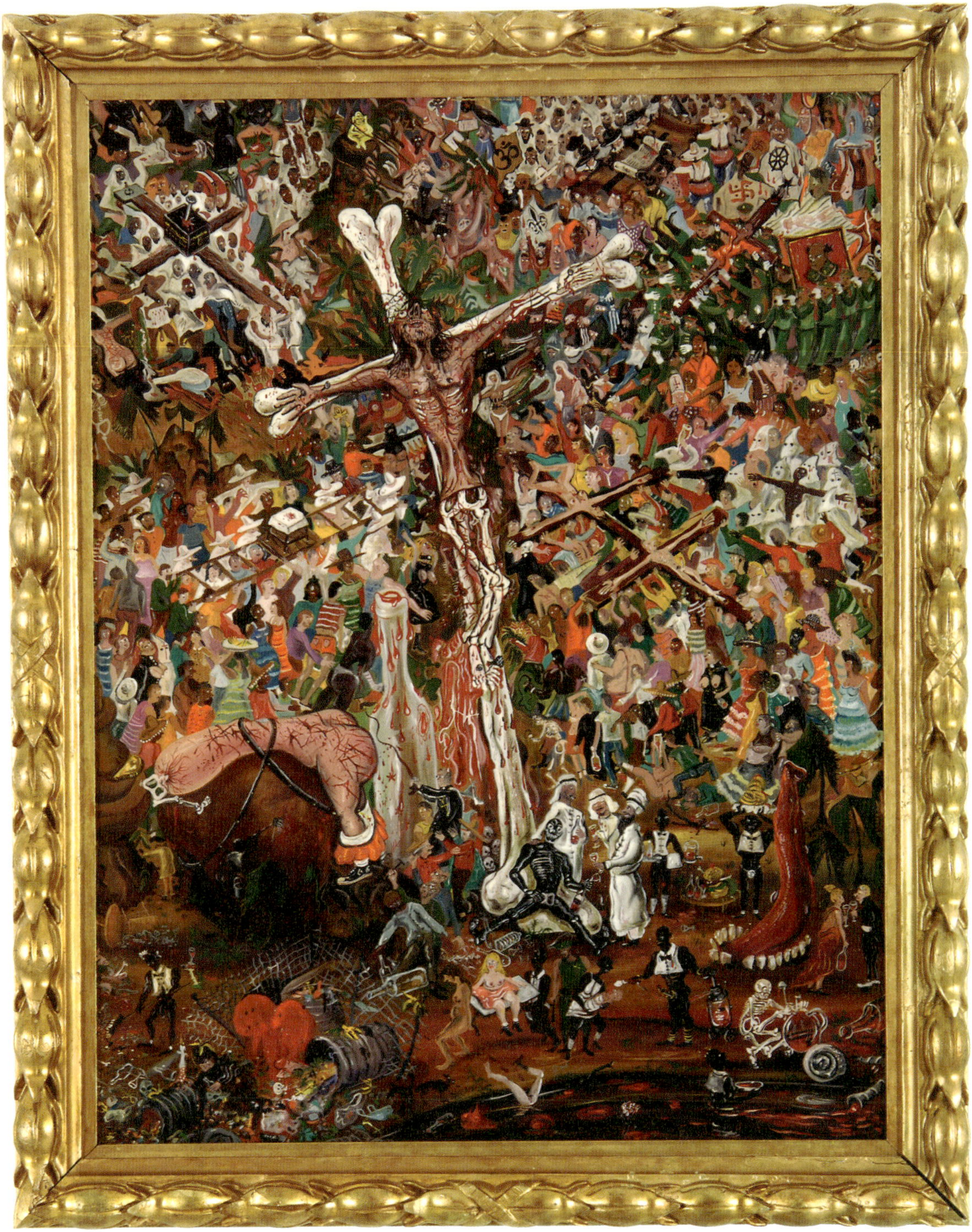

Untitled / Woman in a Cap, 2011

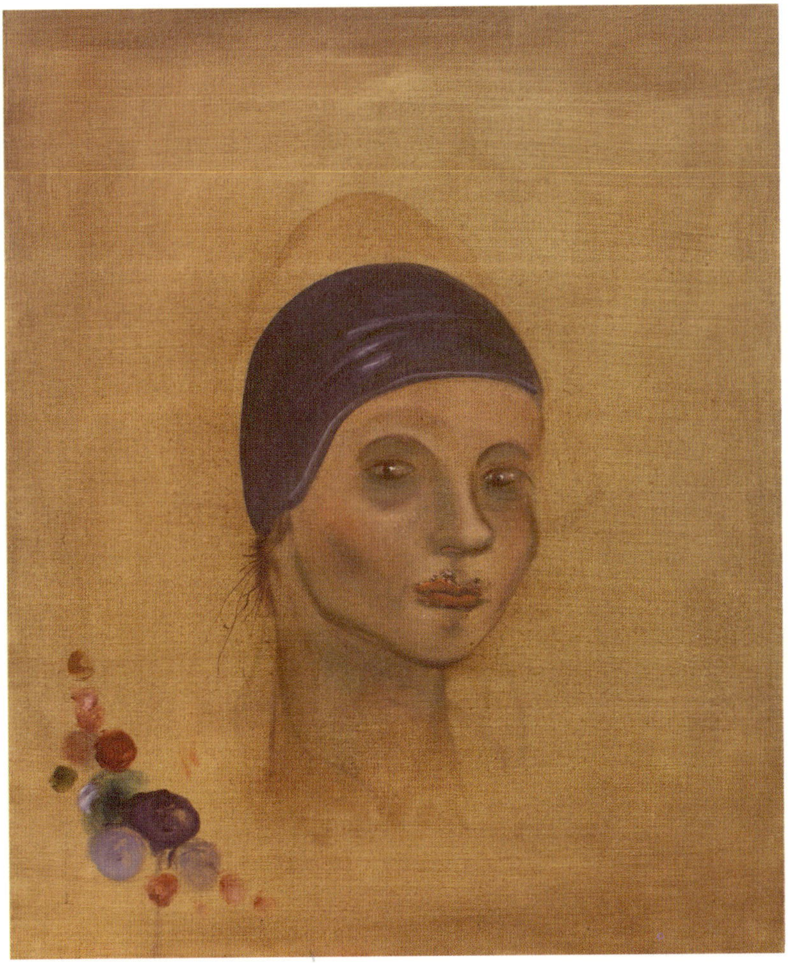

Dark Self Portrait, 2011

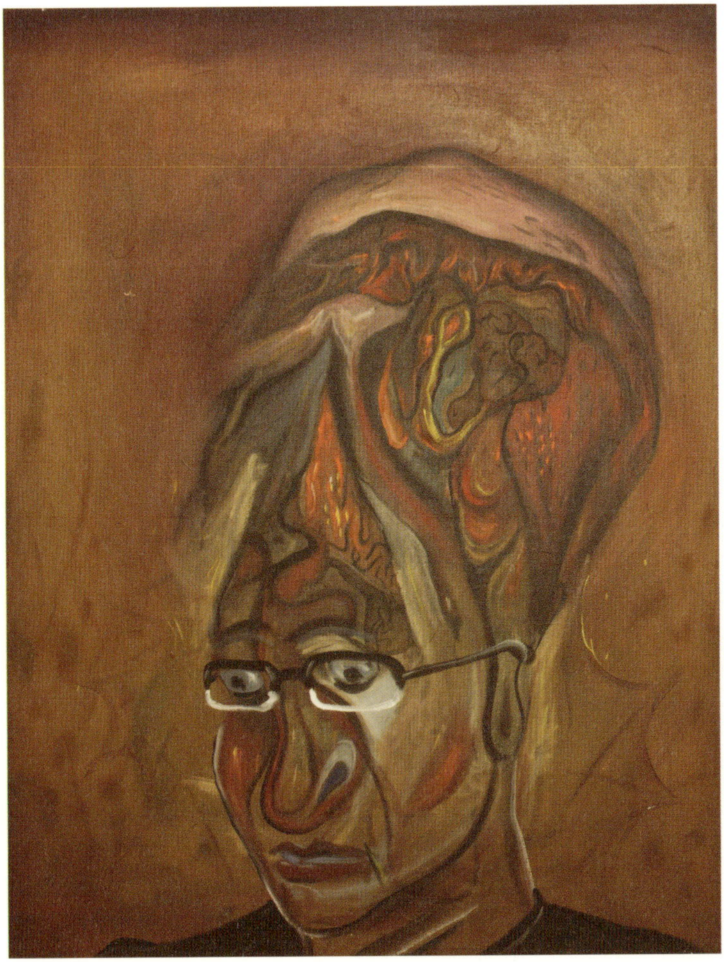

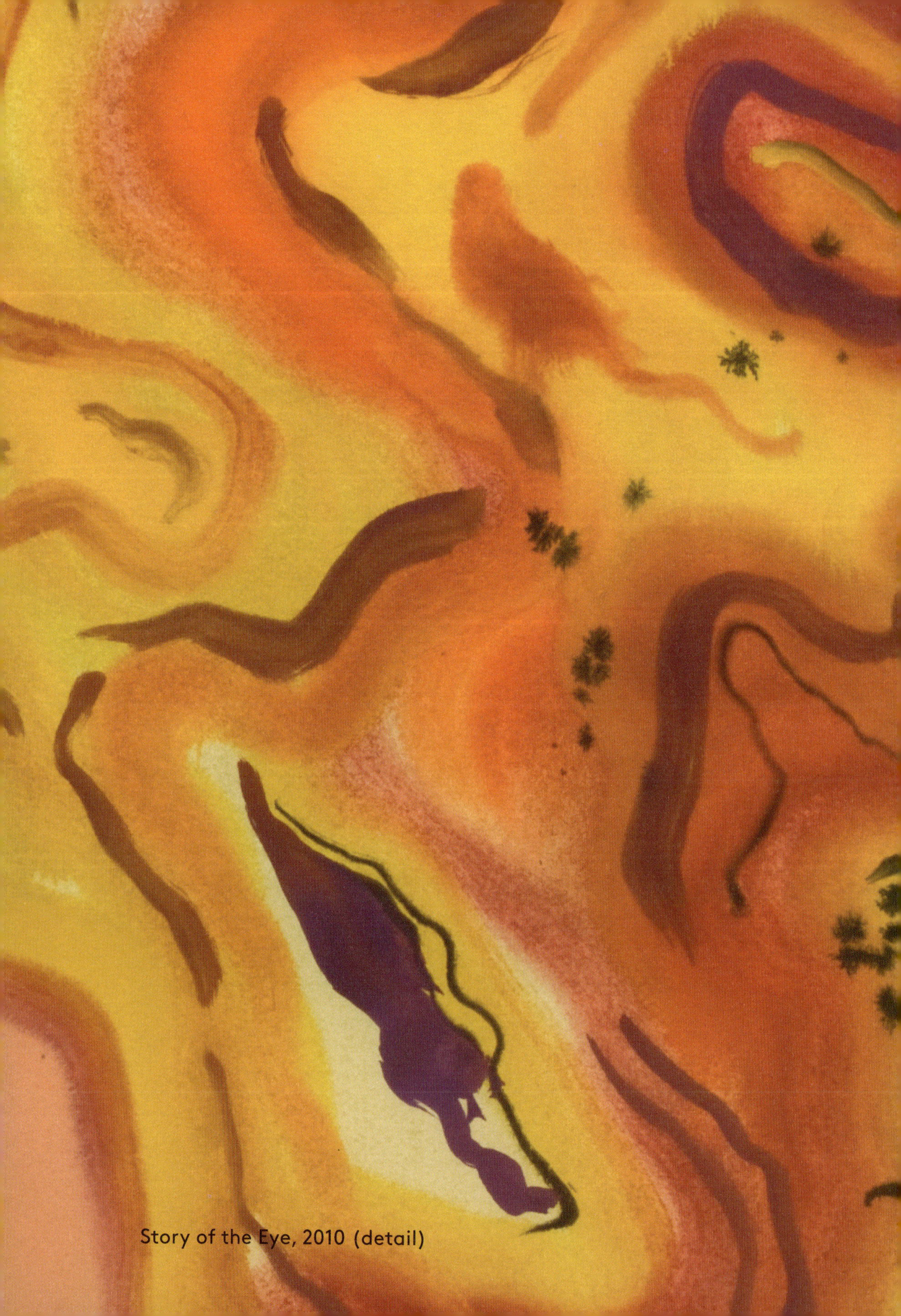

Story of the Eye, 2010 (detail)

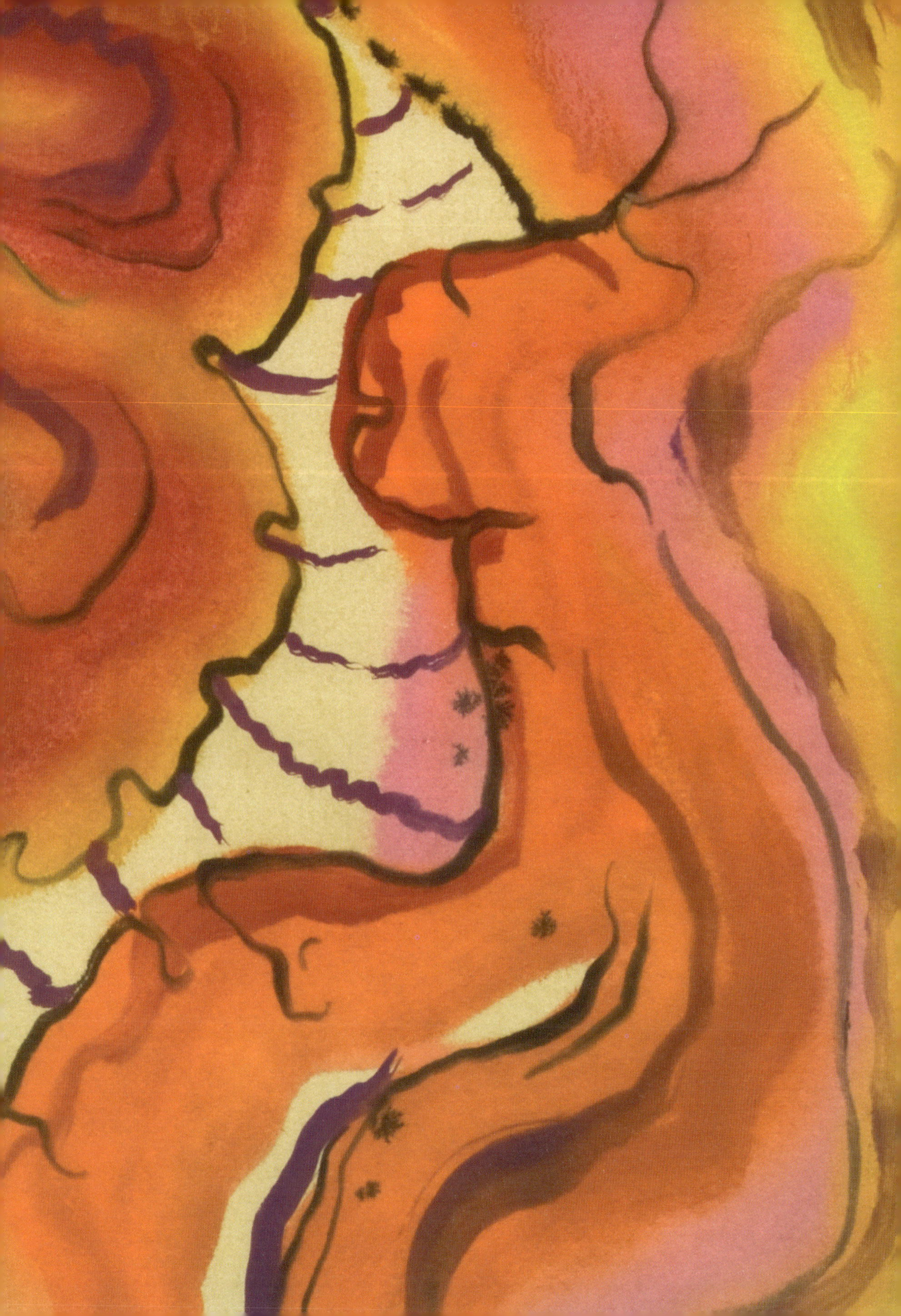

Story of the Eye, 2010

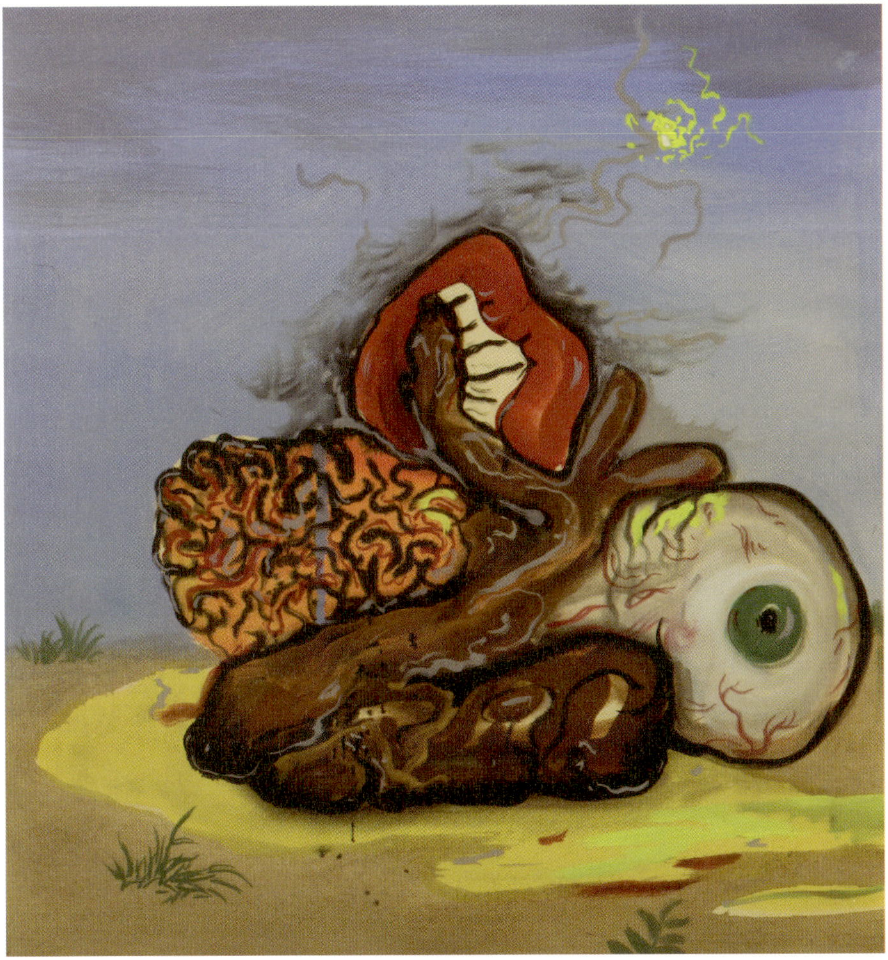

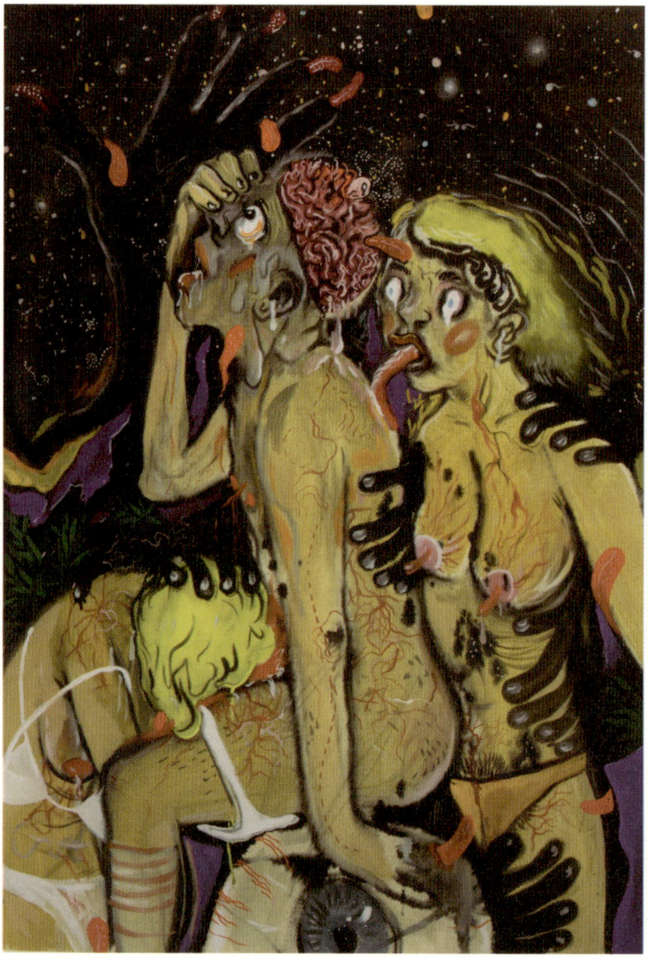

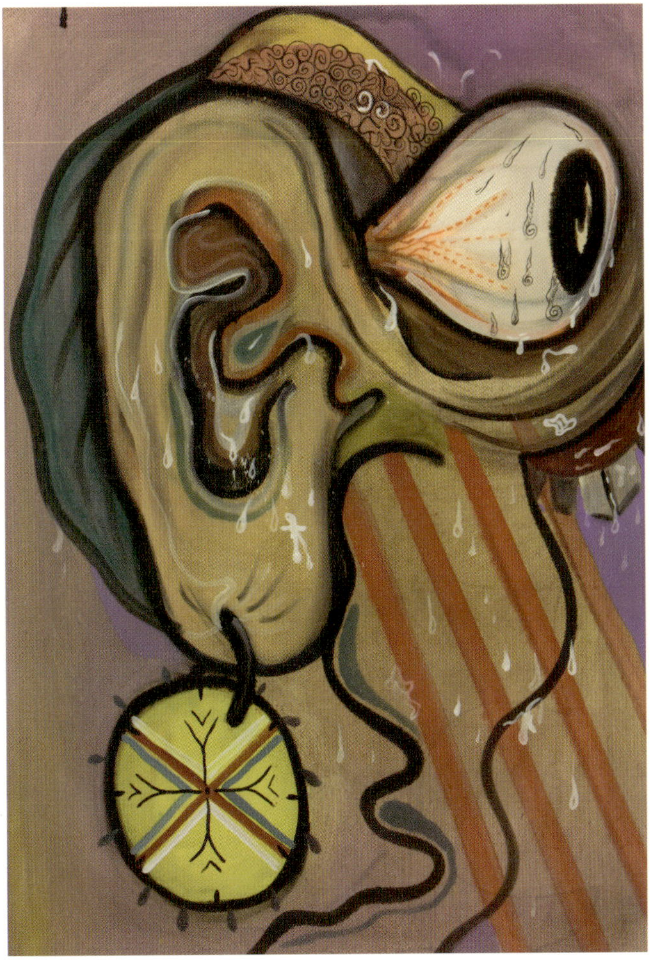

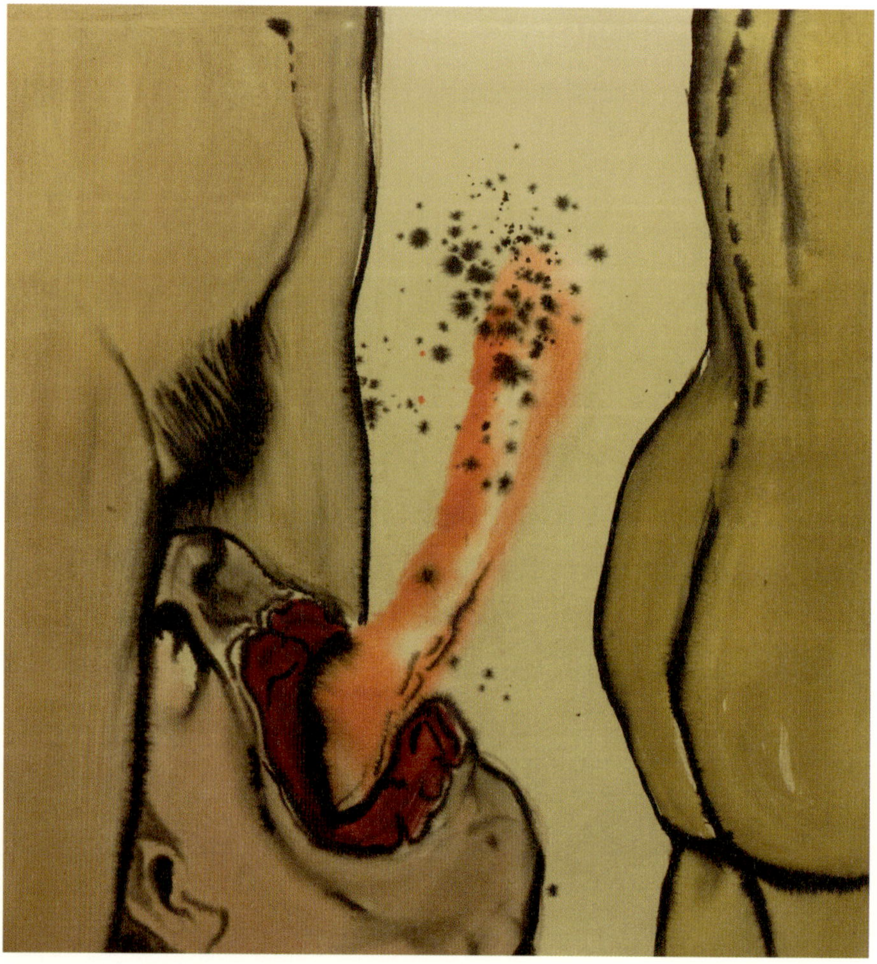

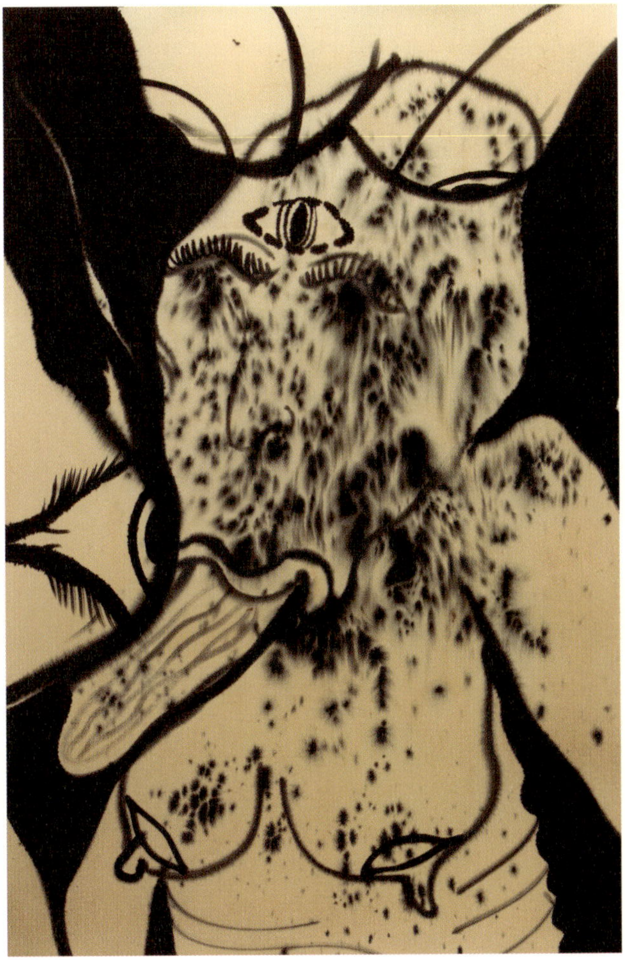

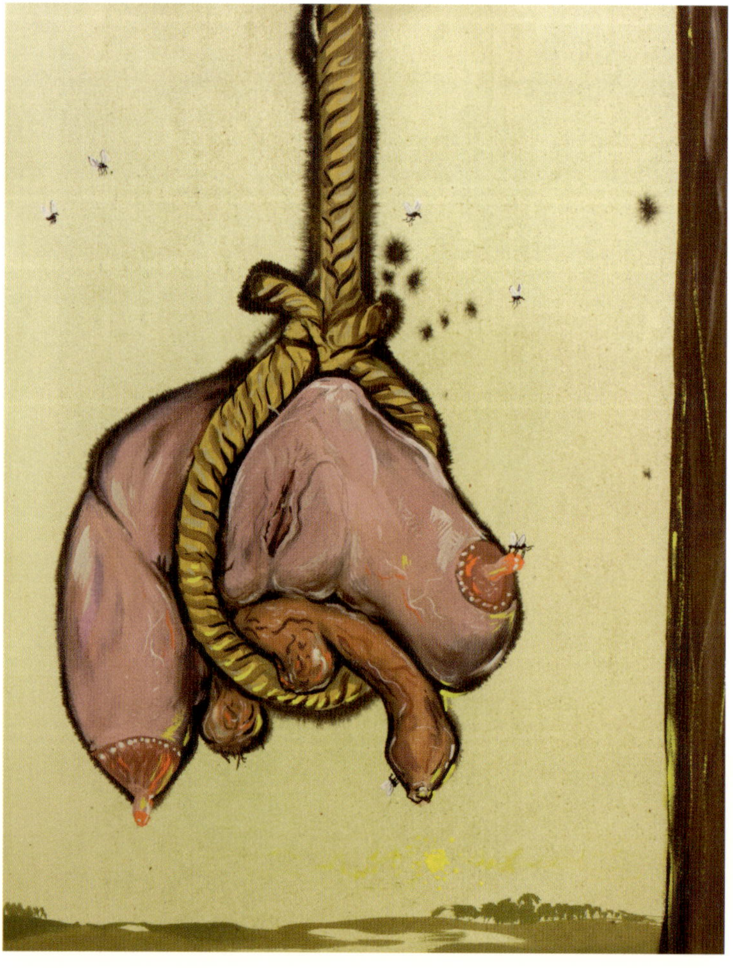

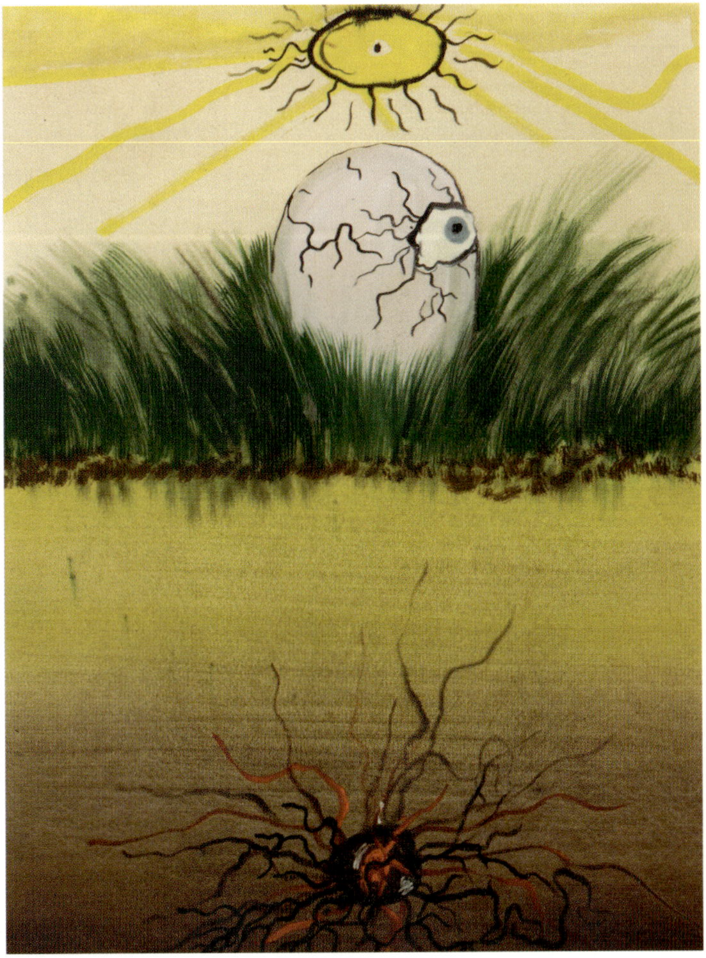

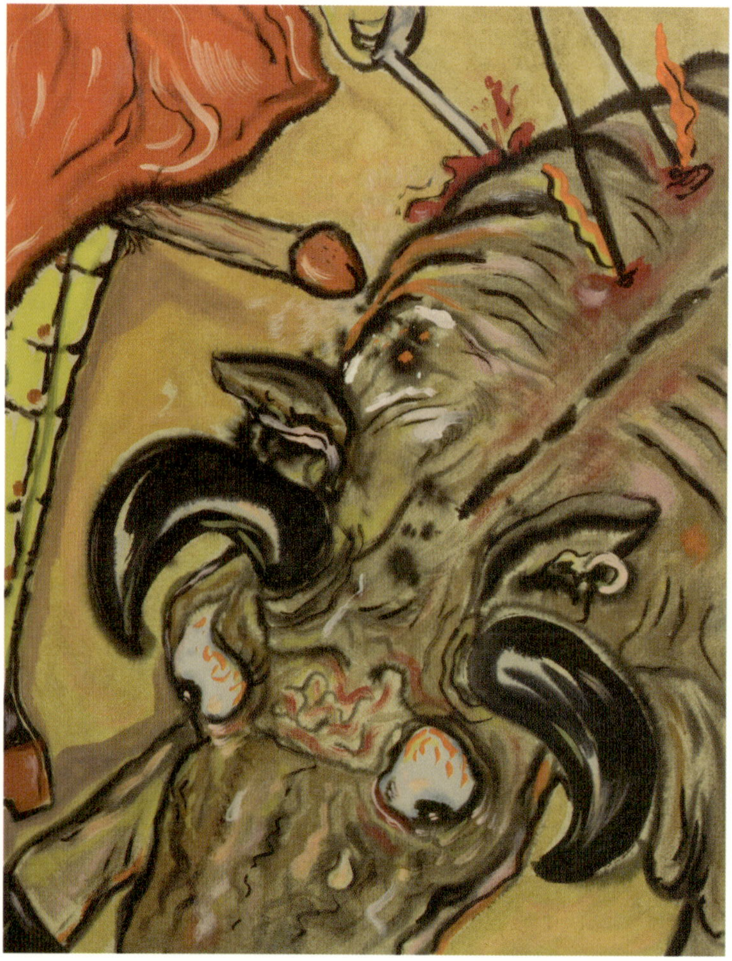

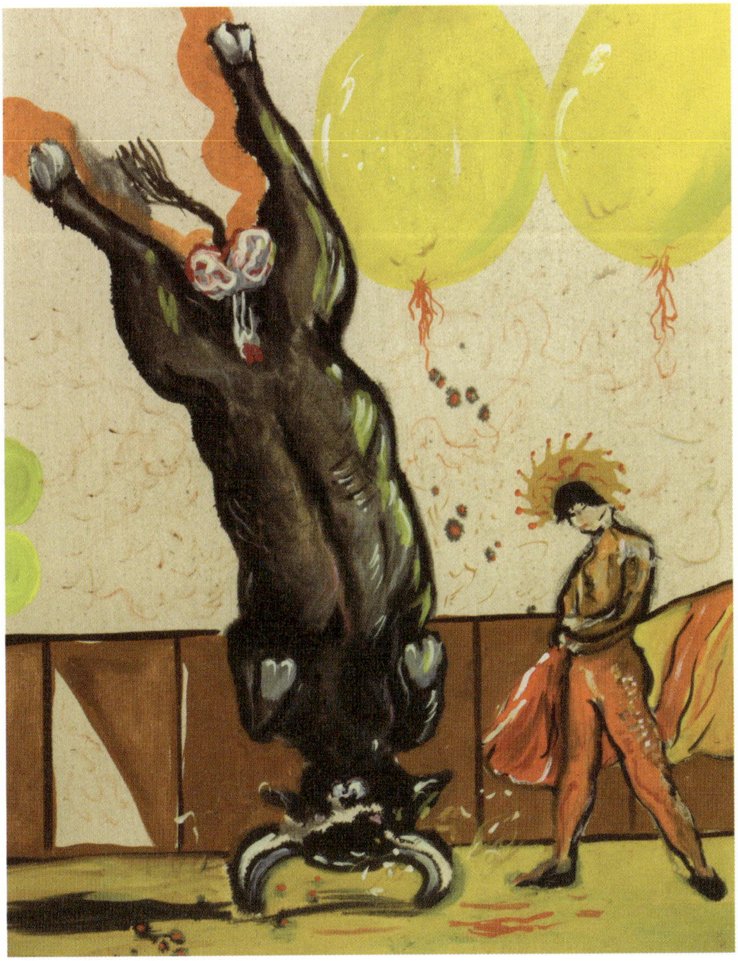

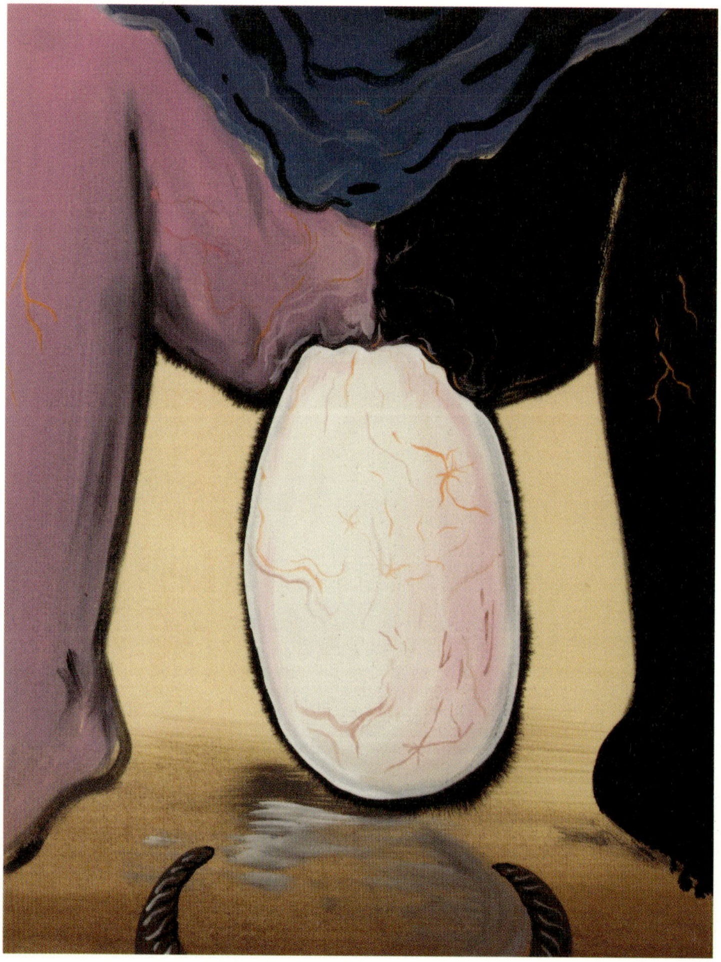

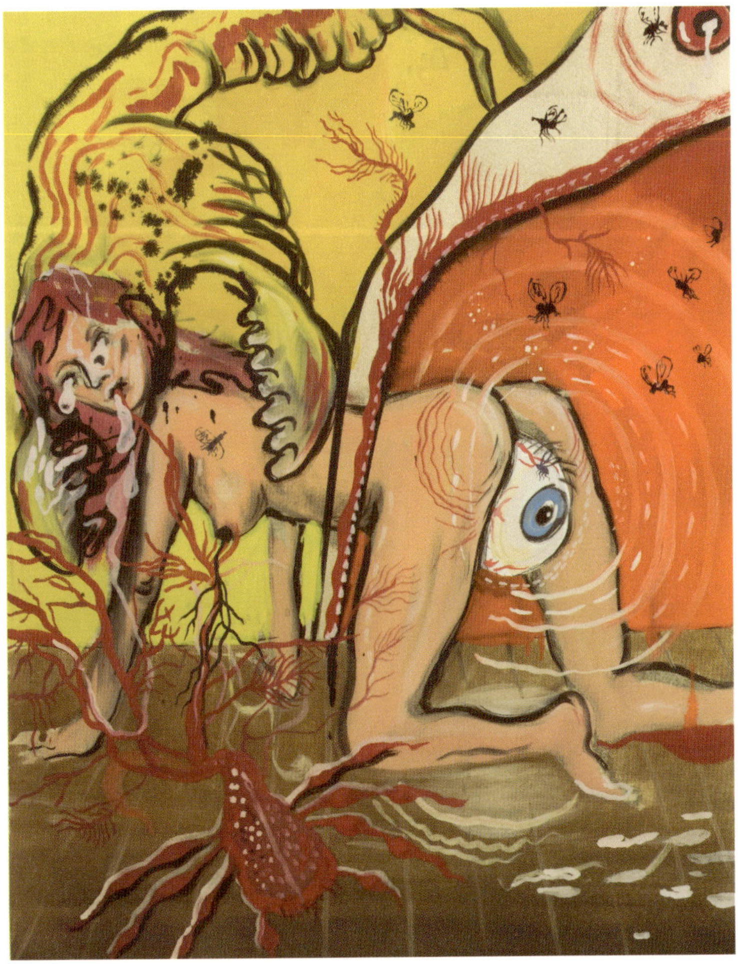

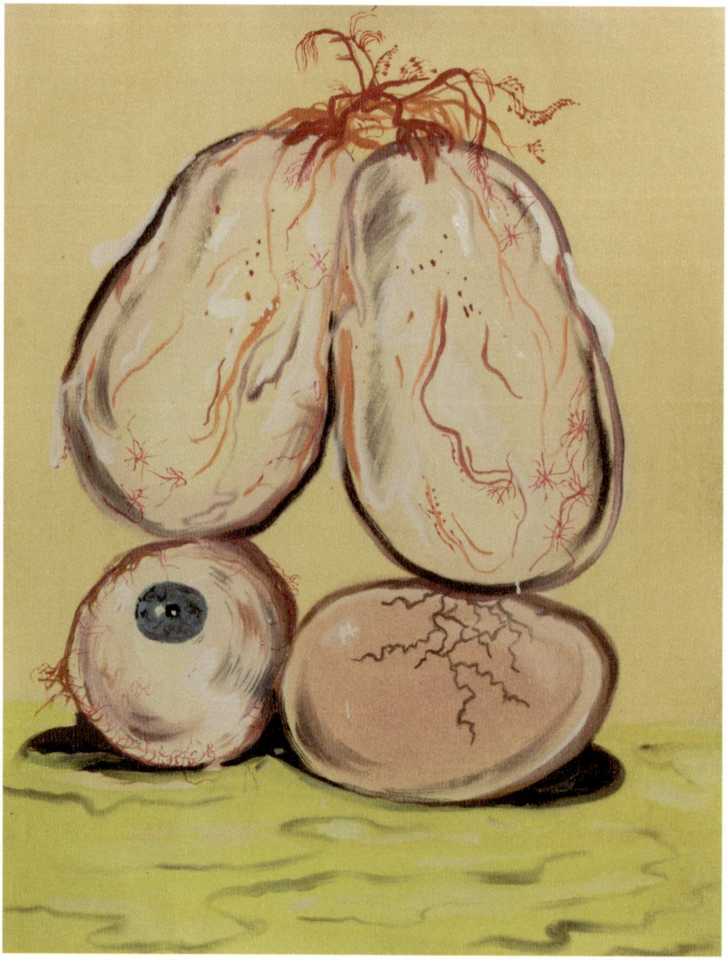

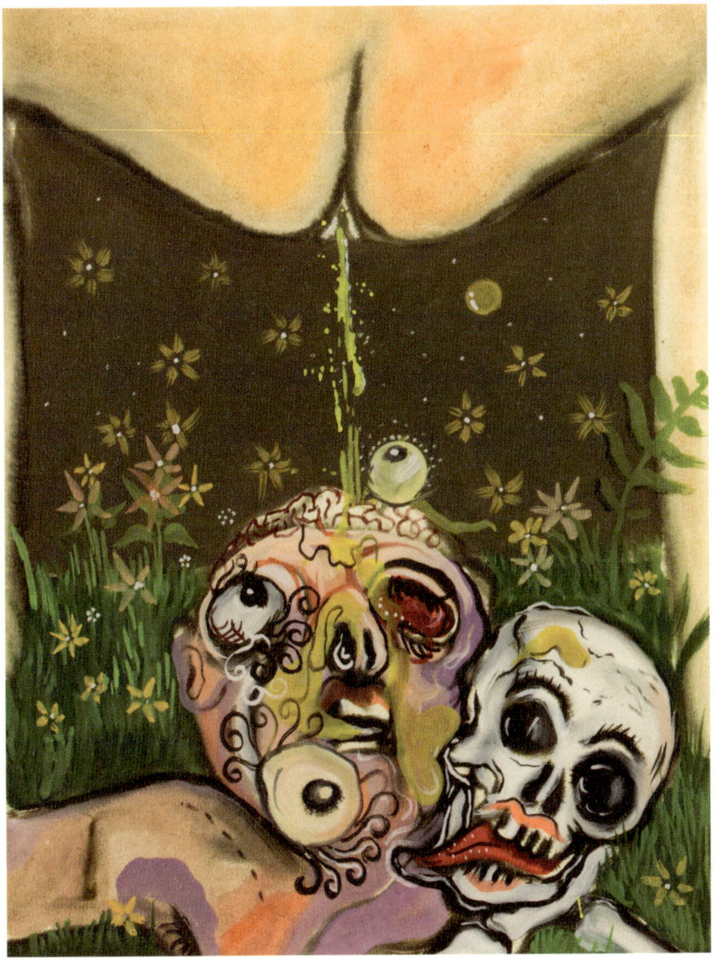

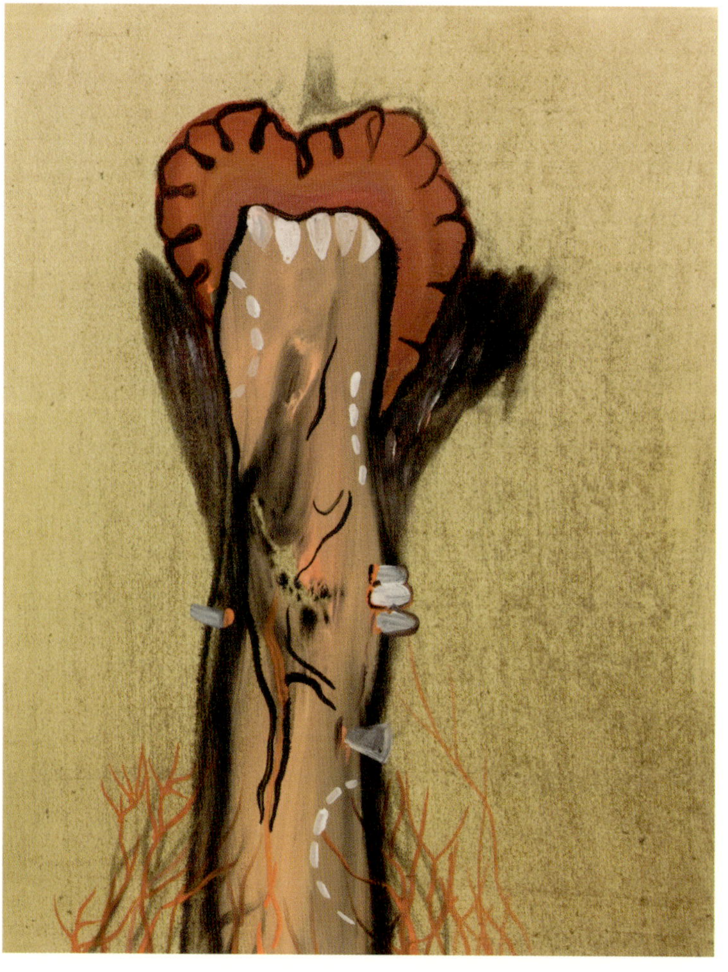

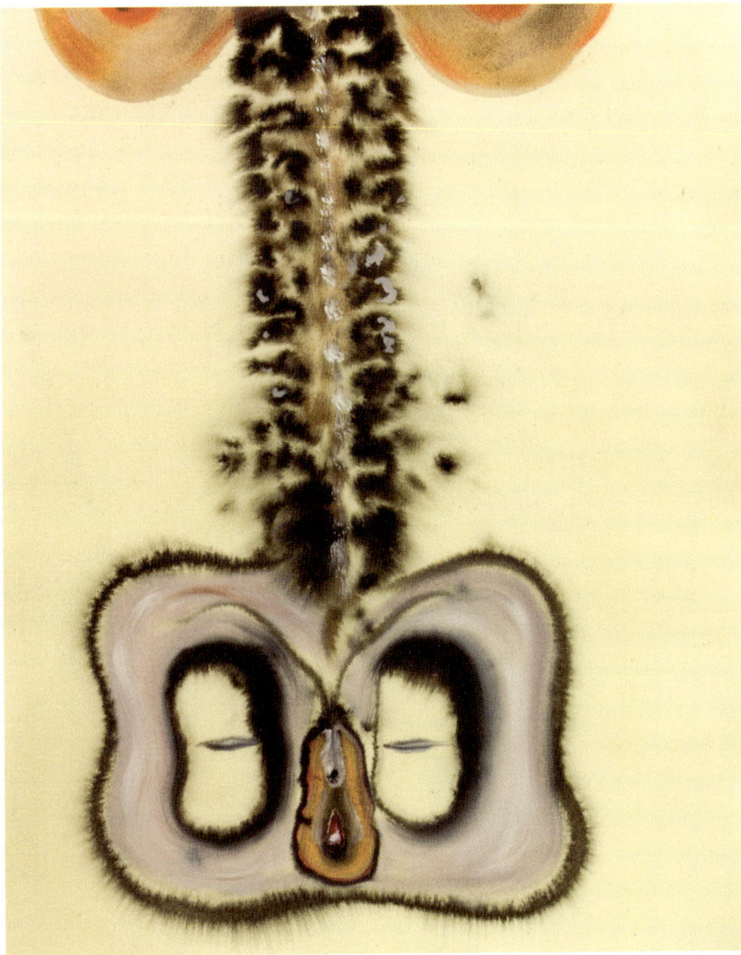

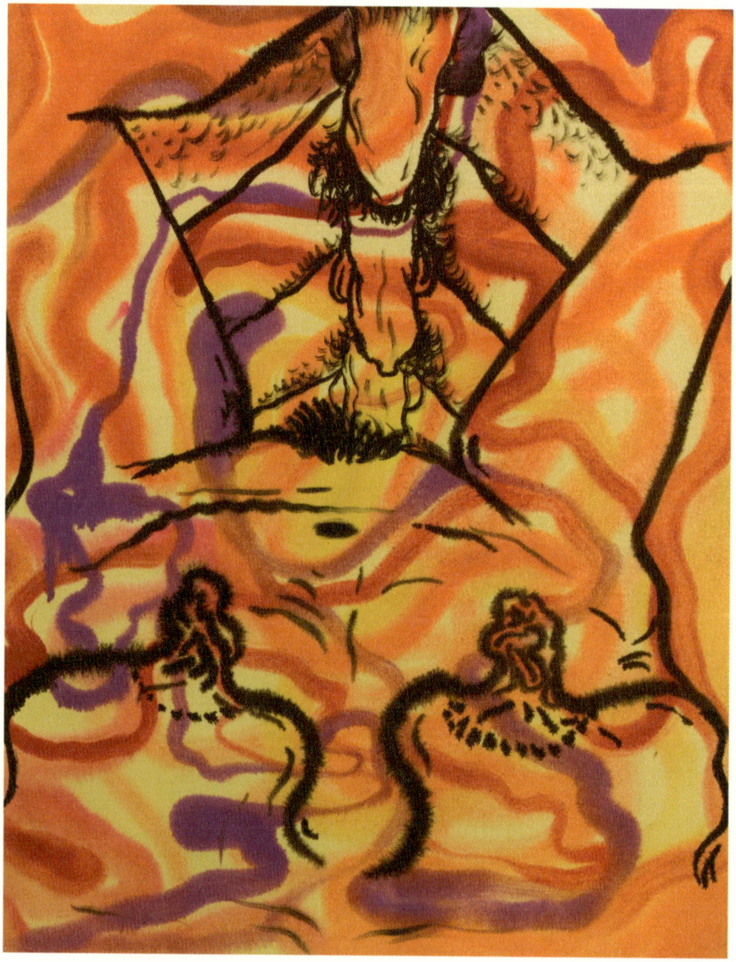

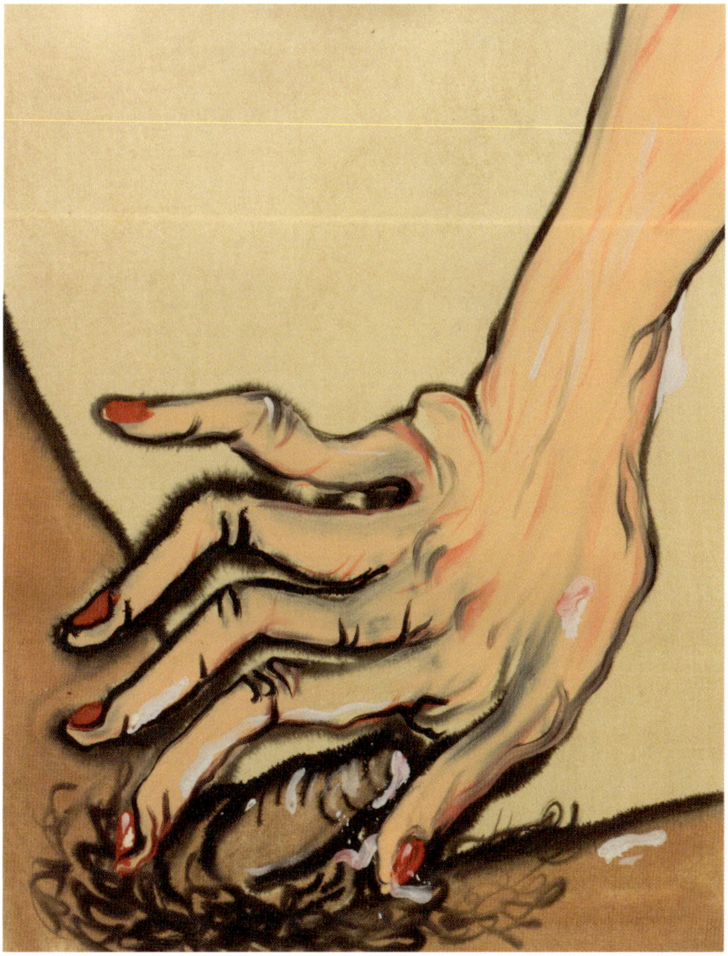

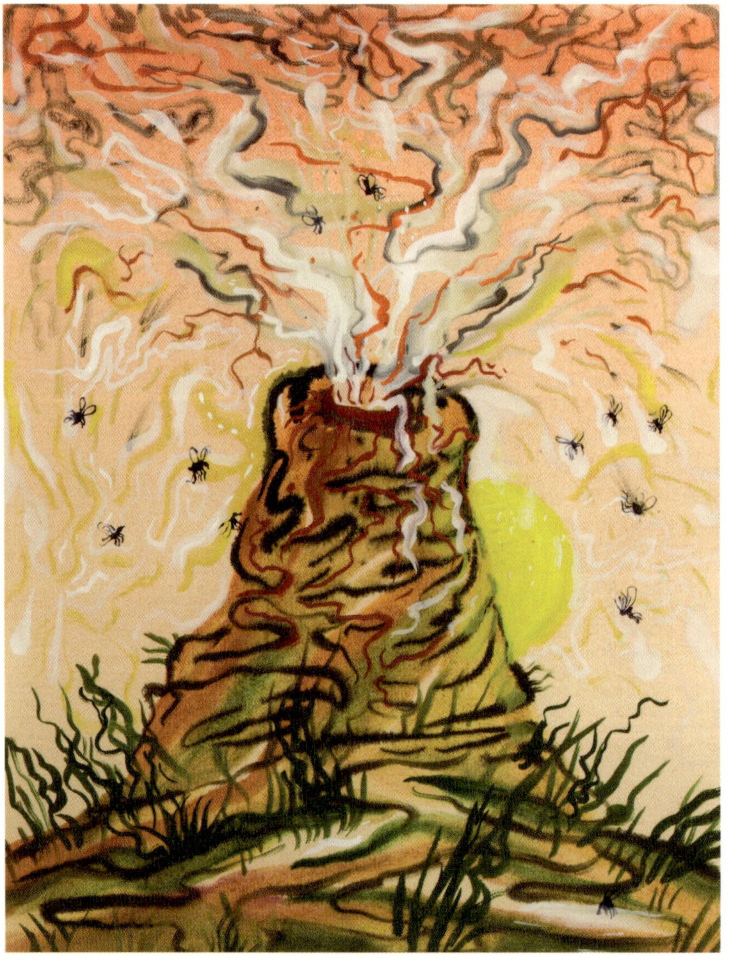

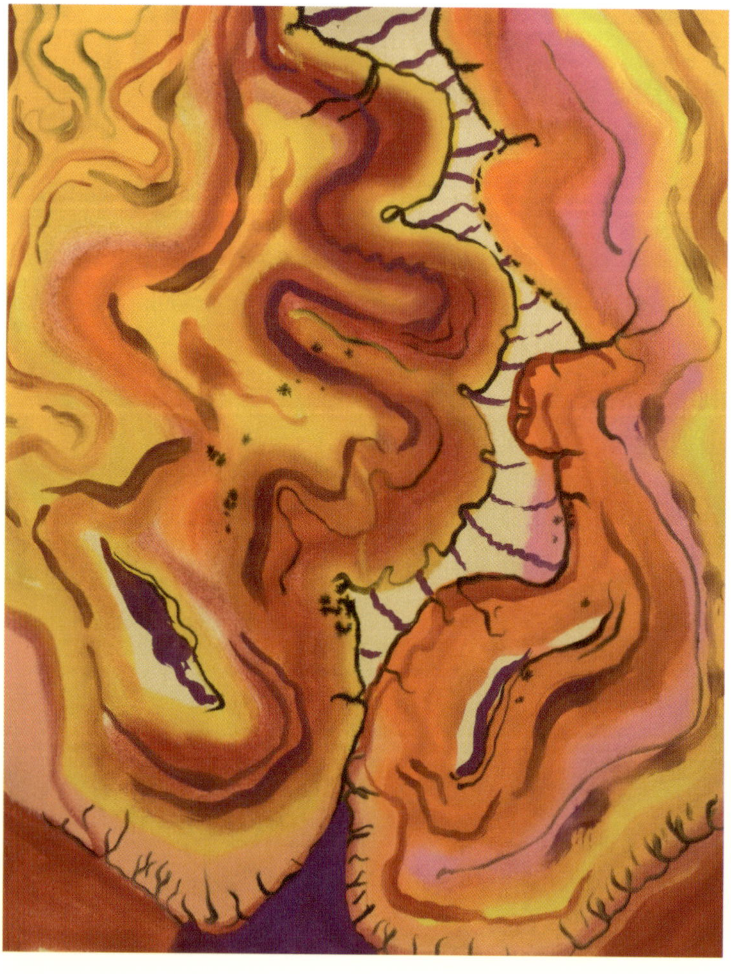

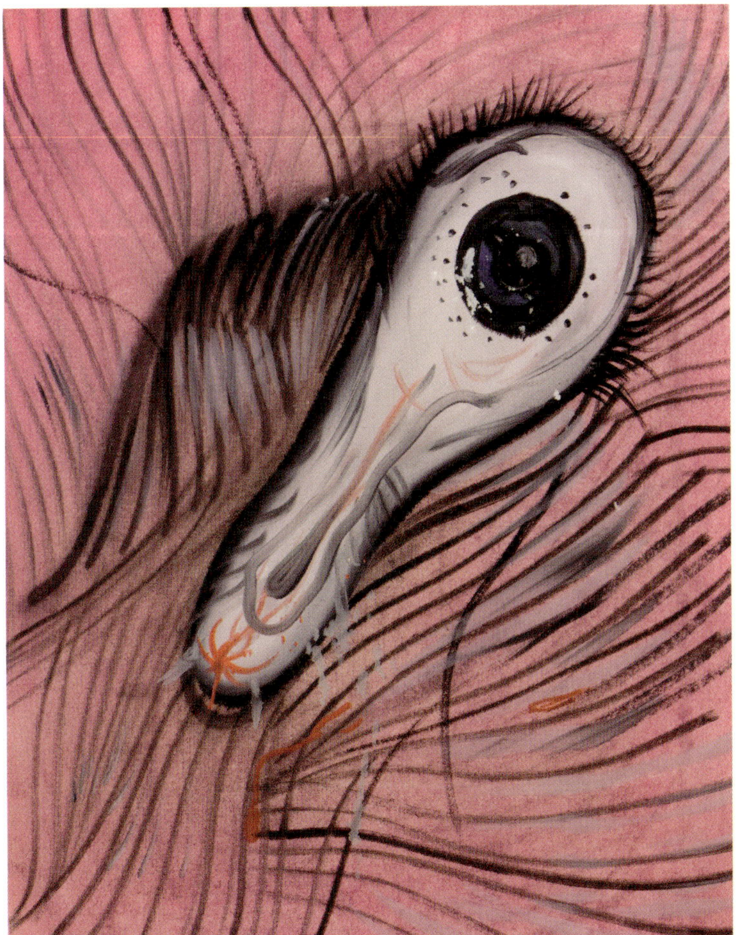

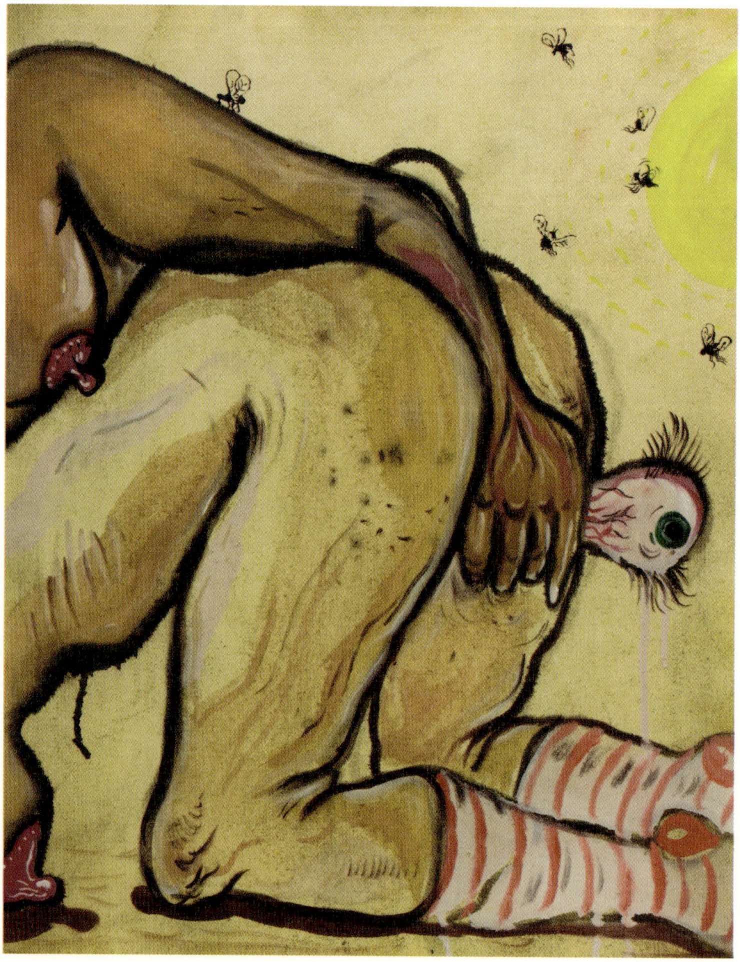

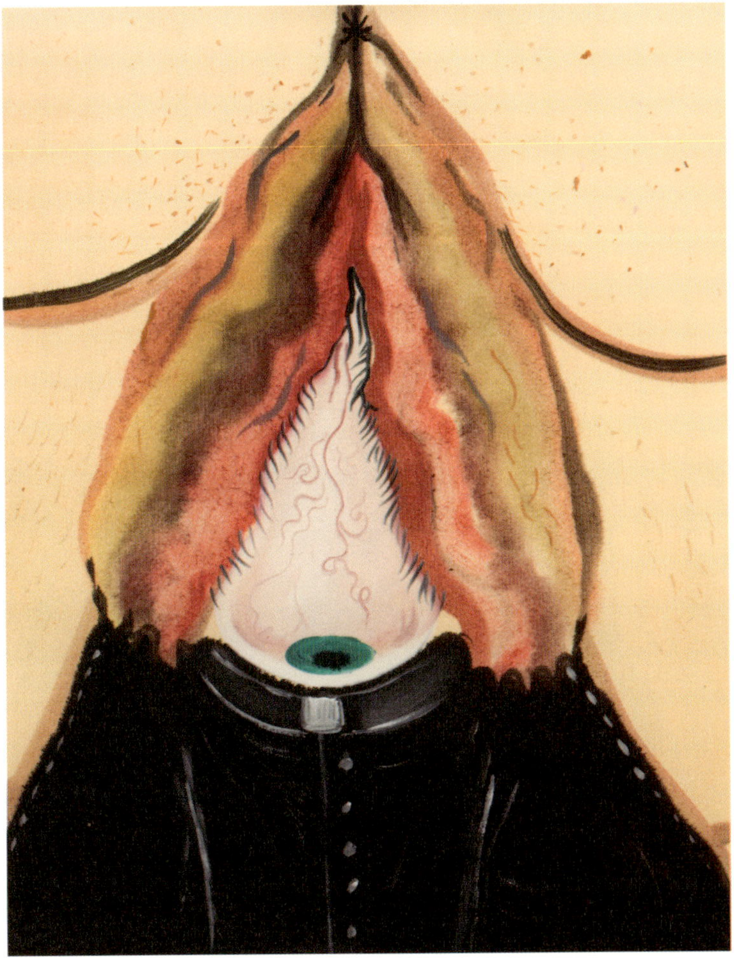

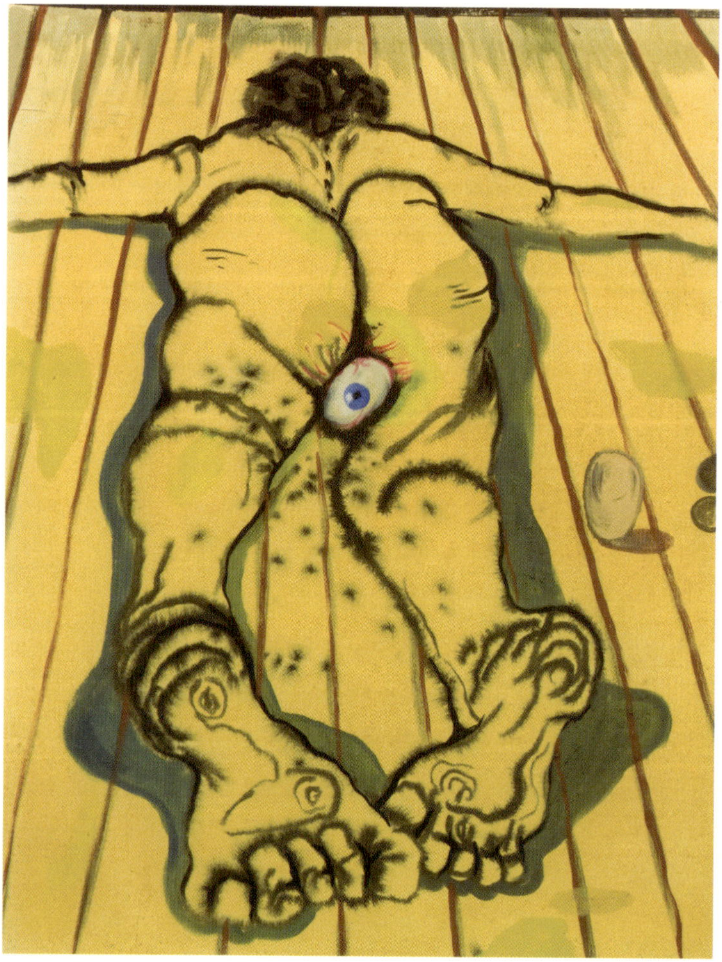

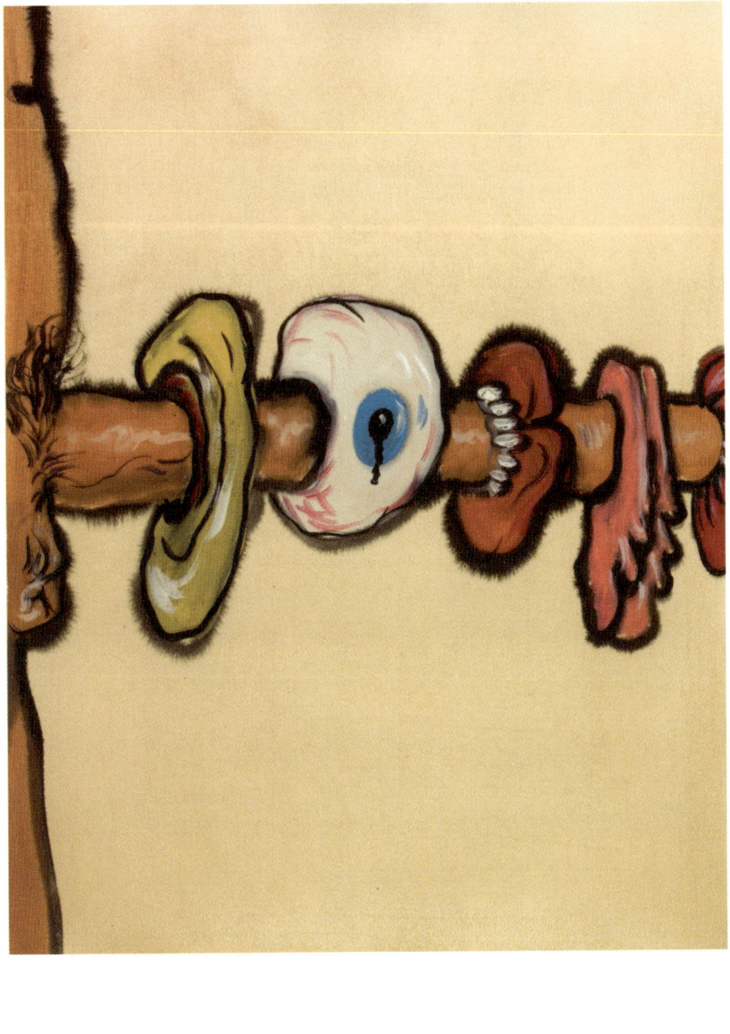

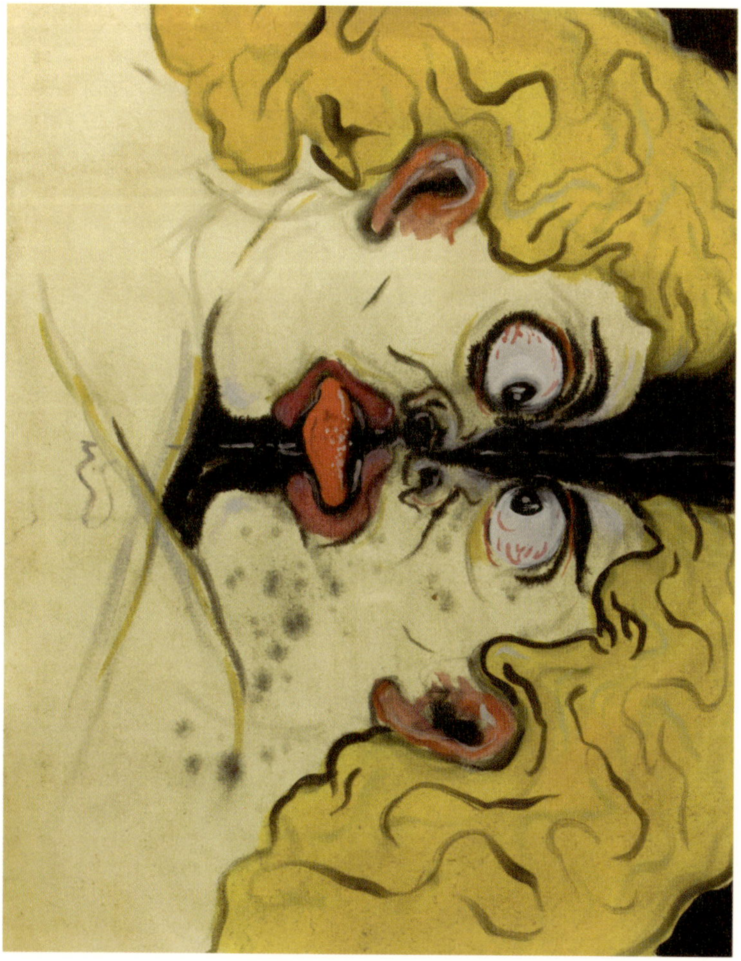

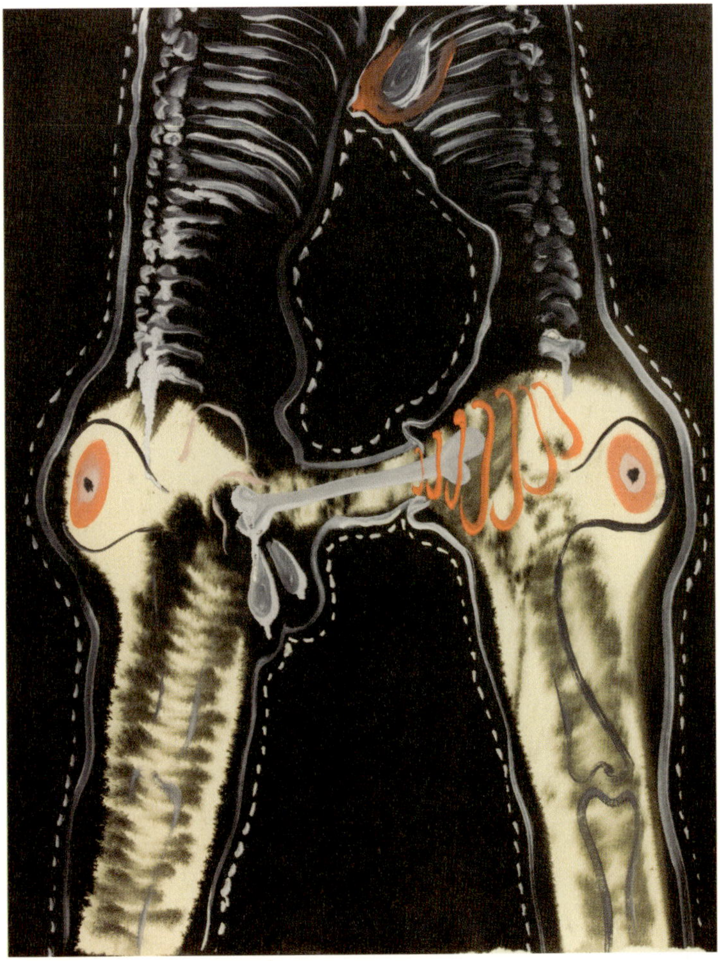

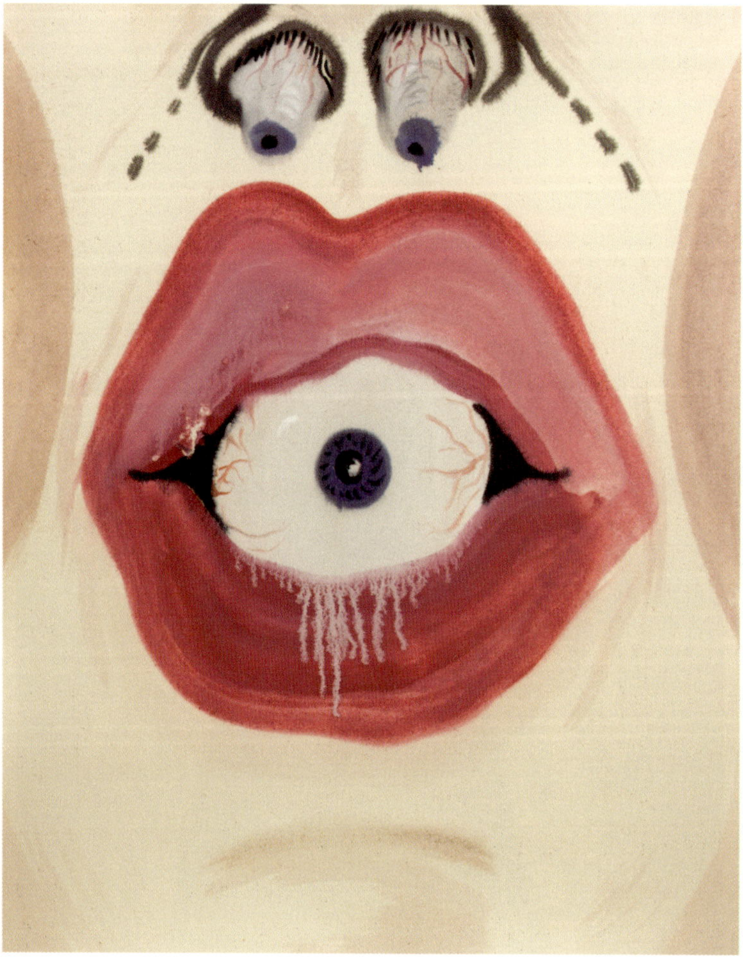

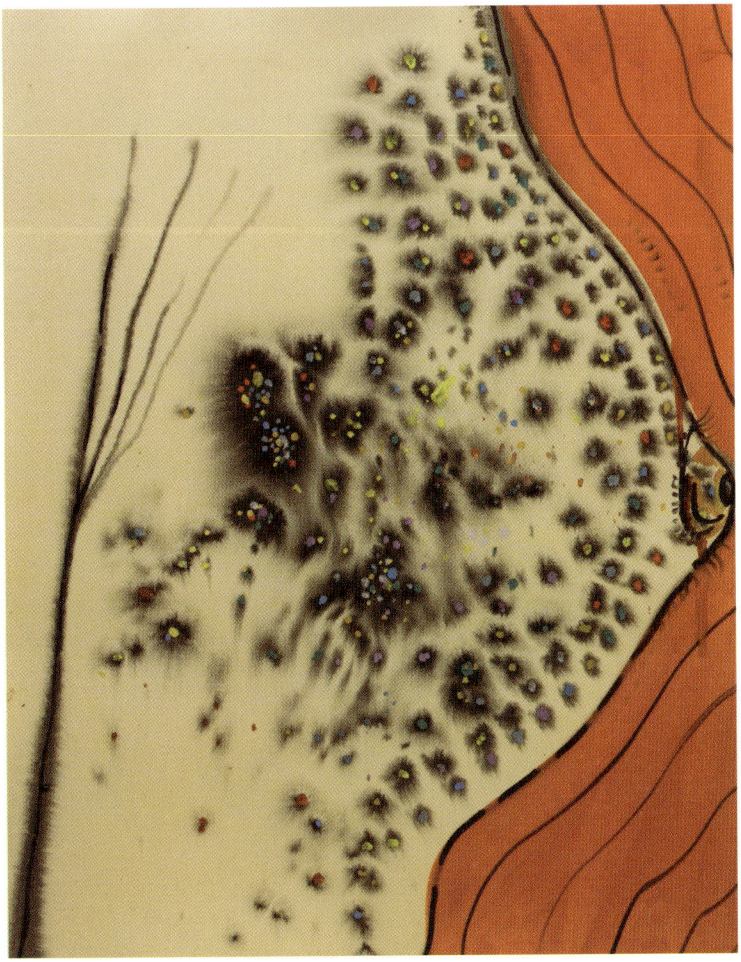

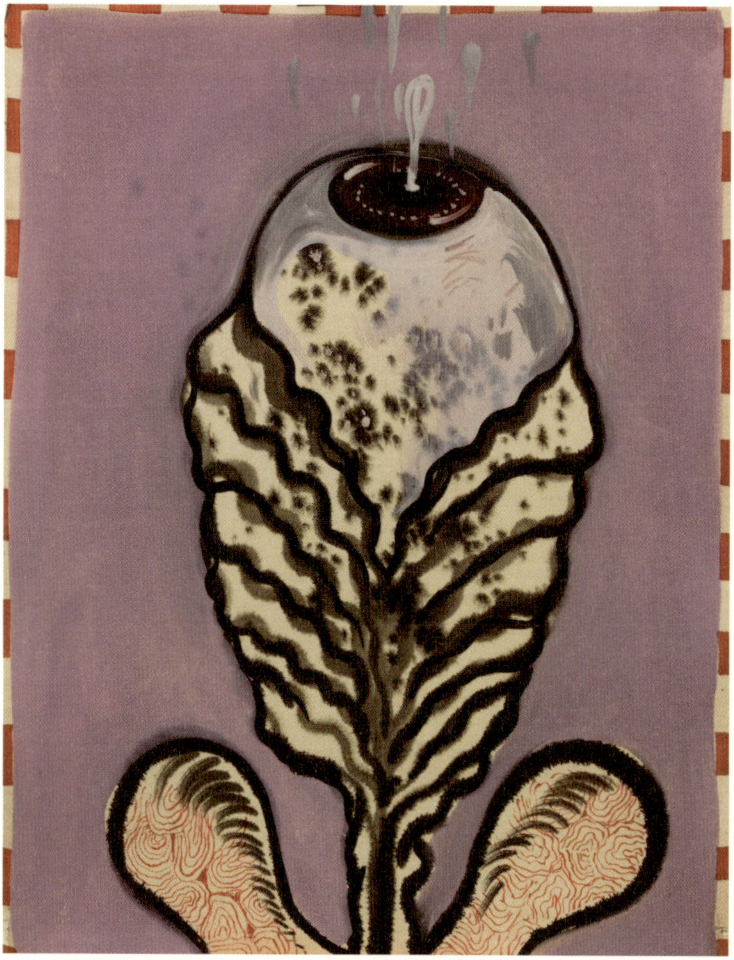

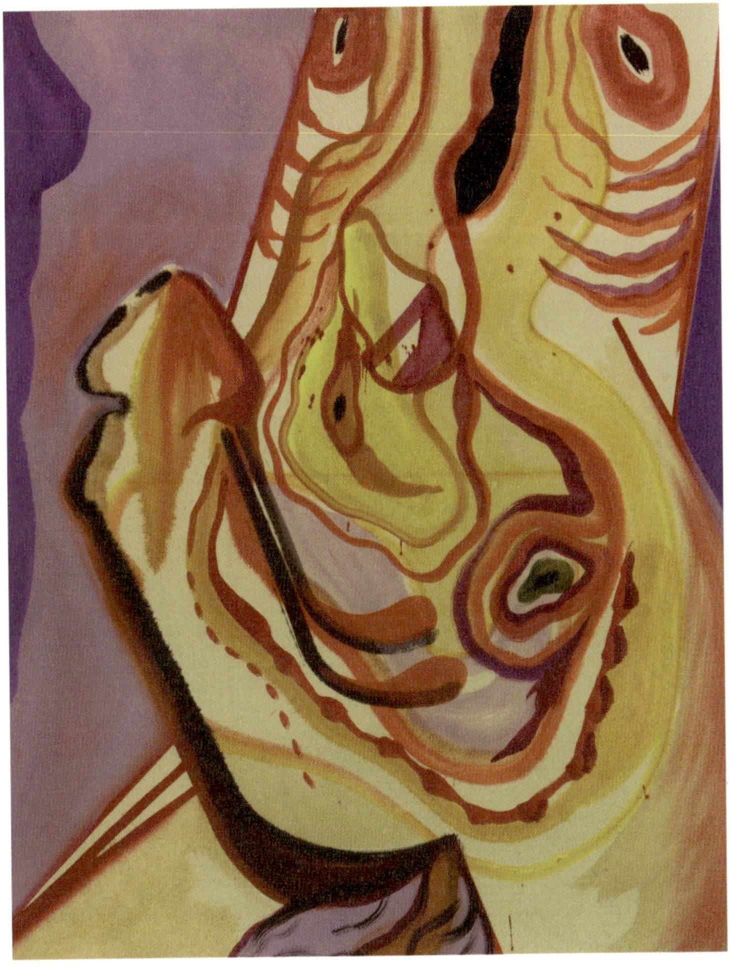

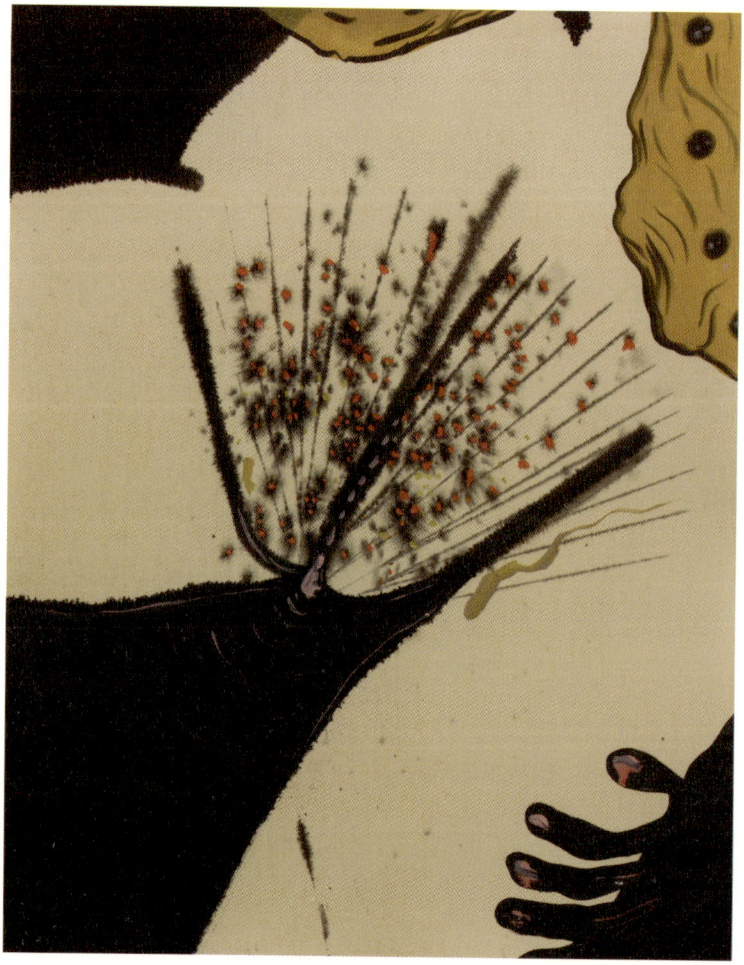

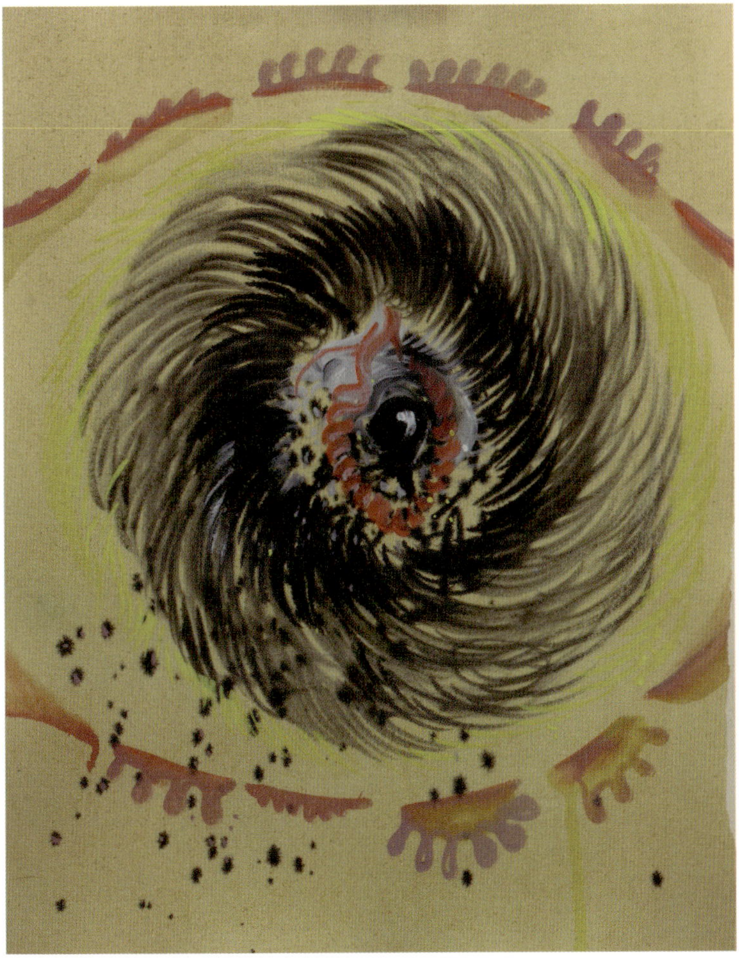

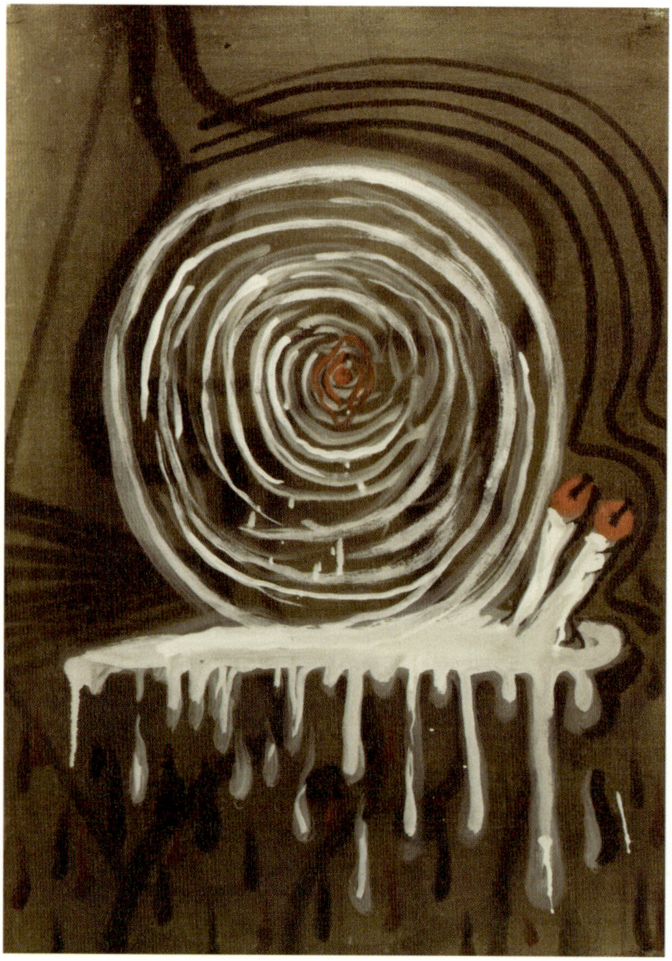

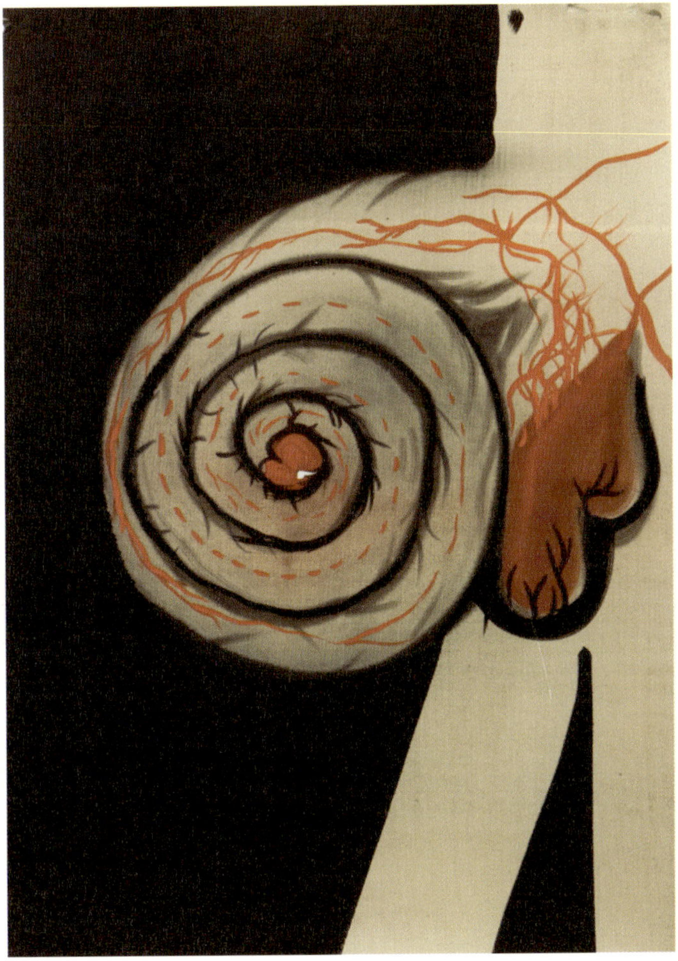

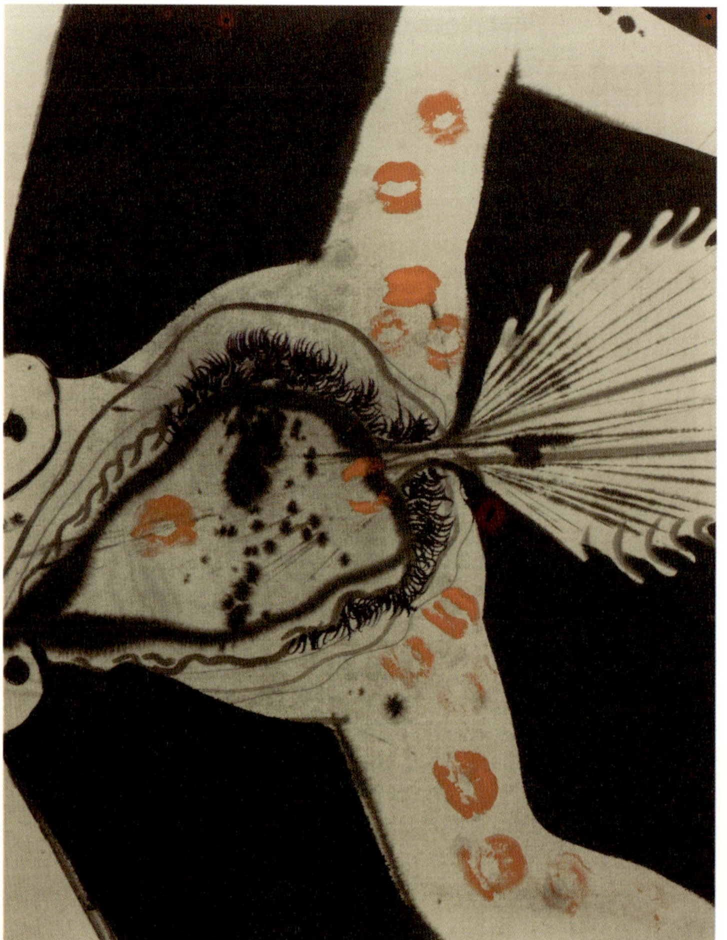

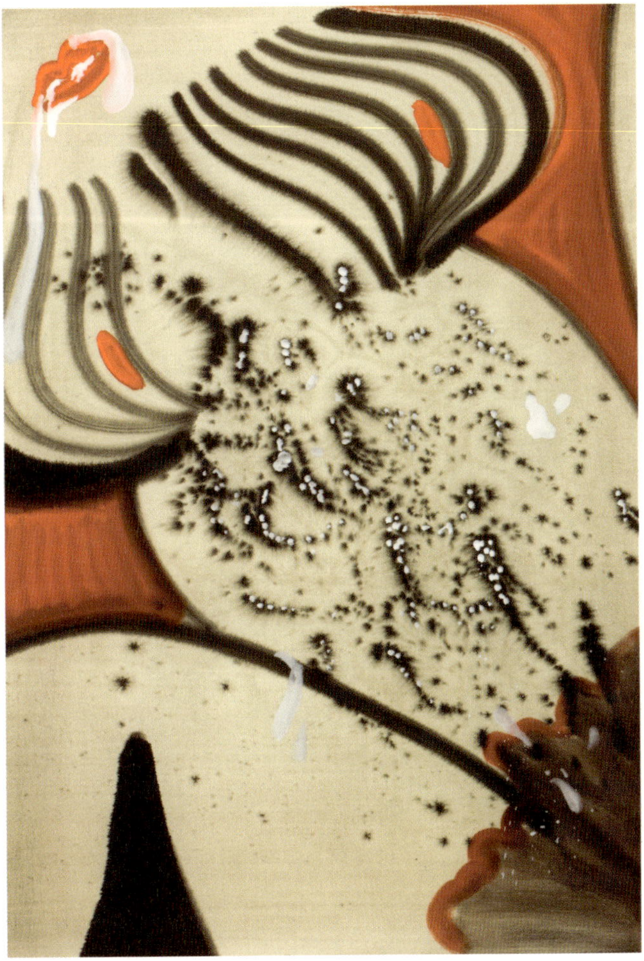

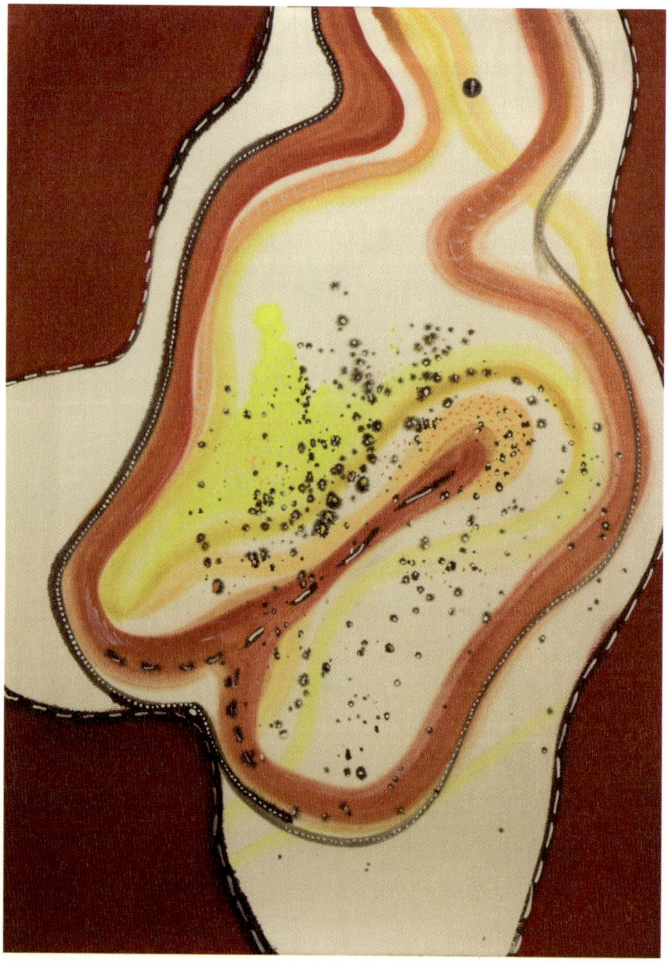

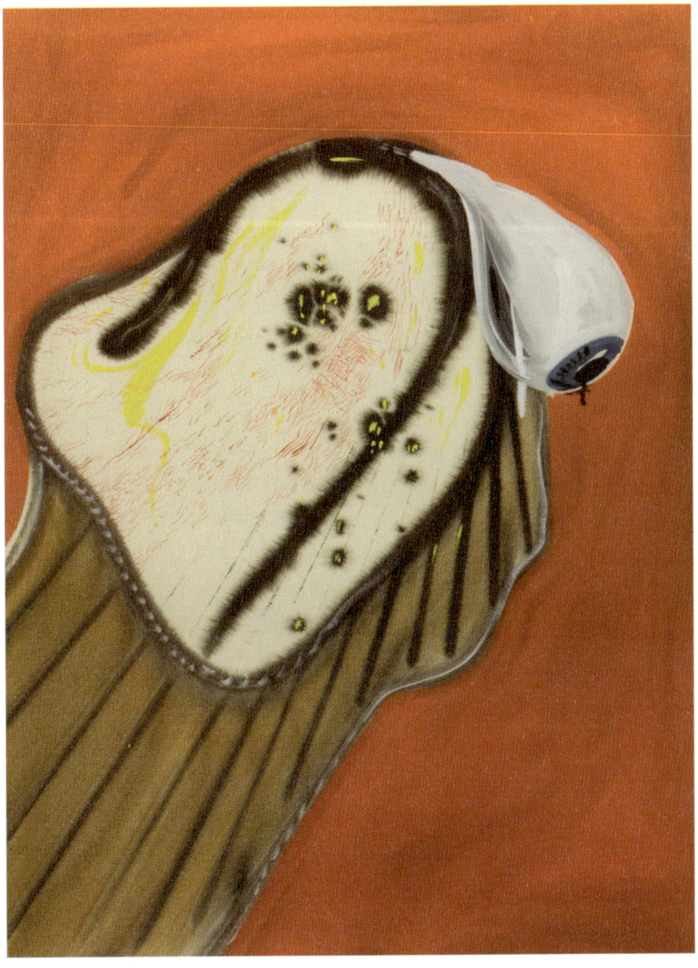

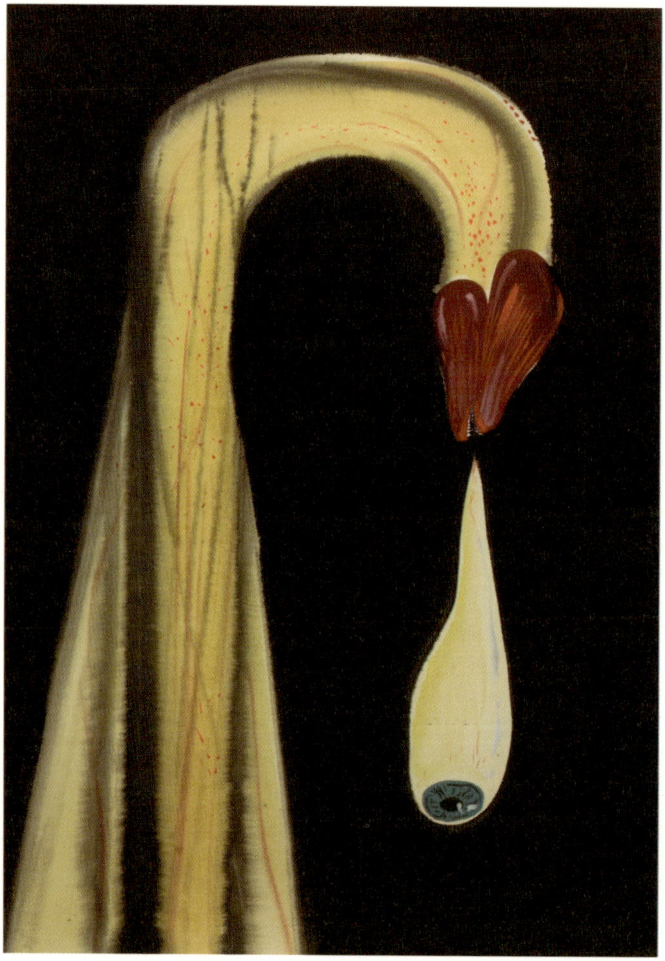

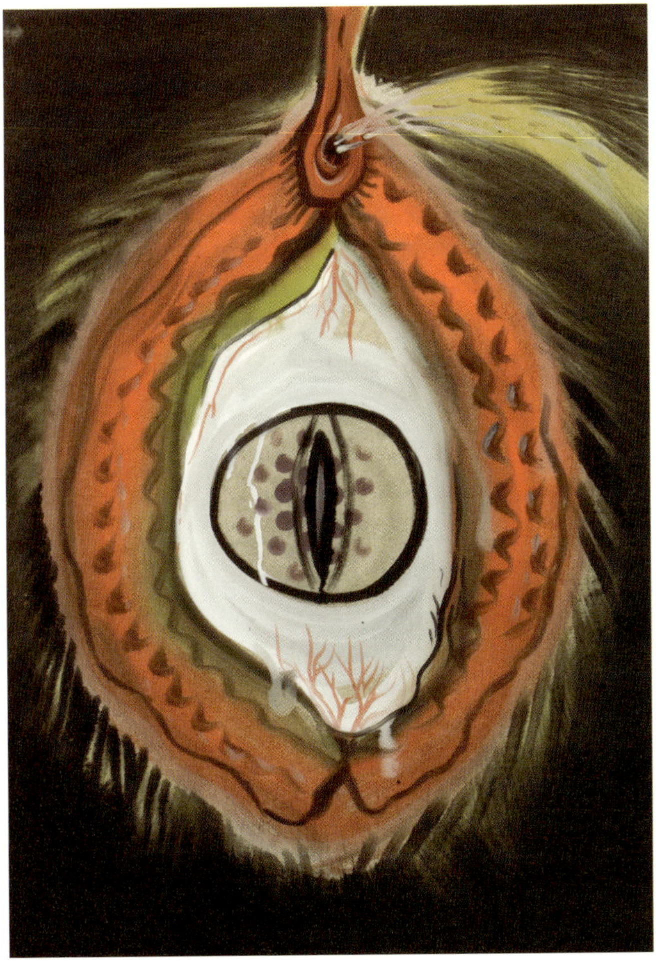

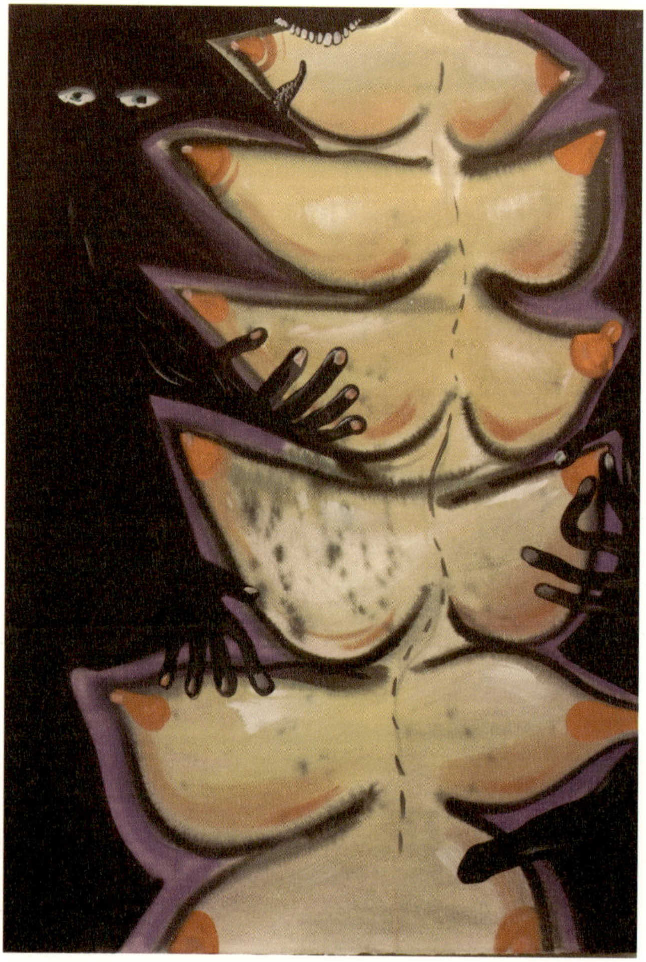

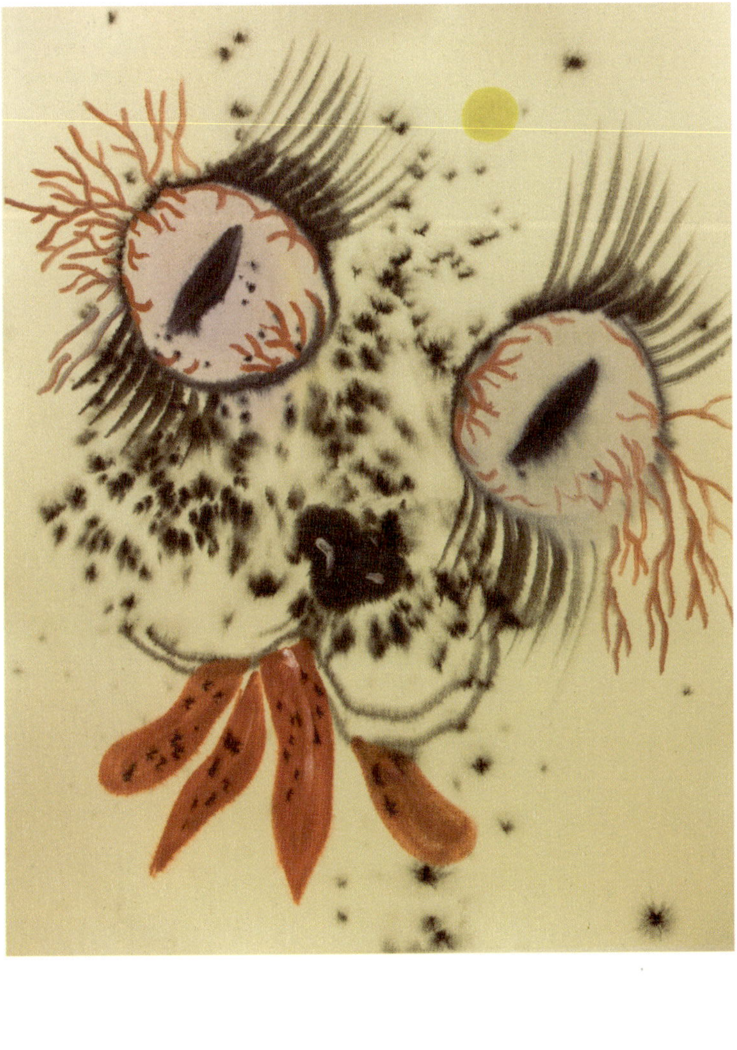

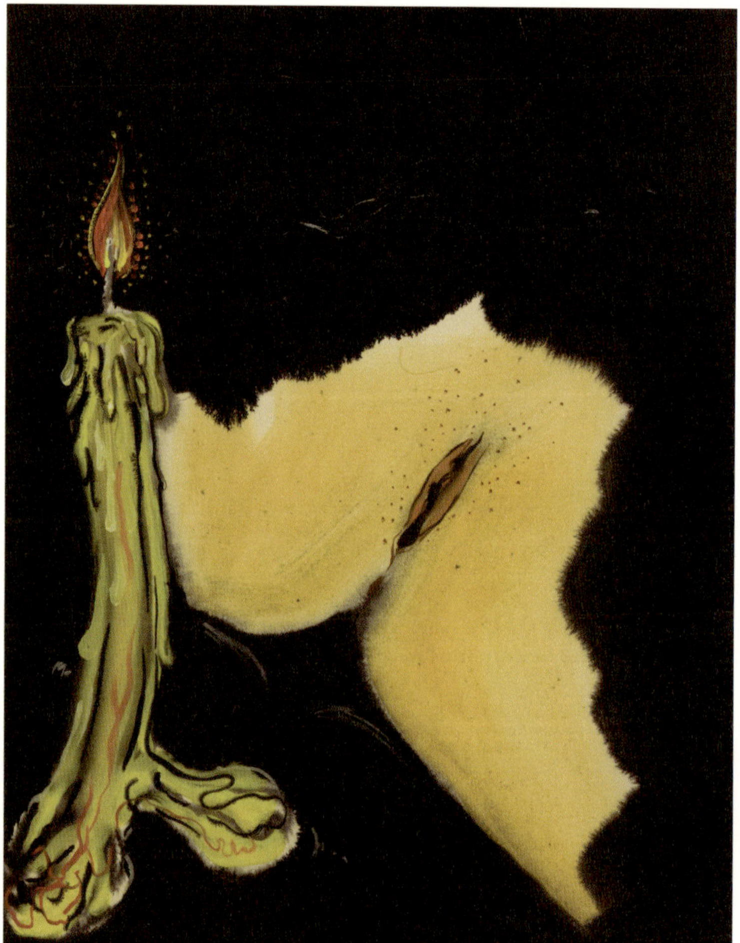

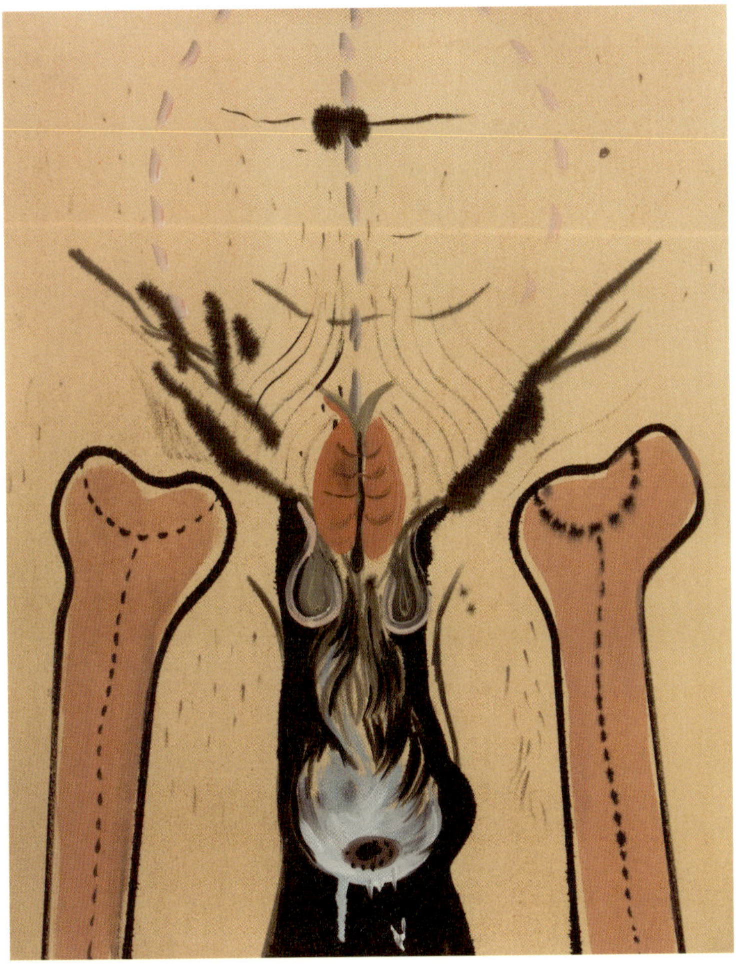

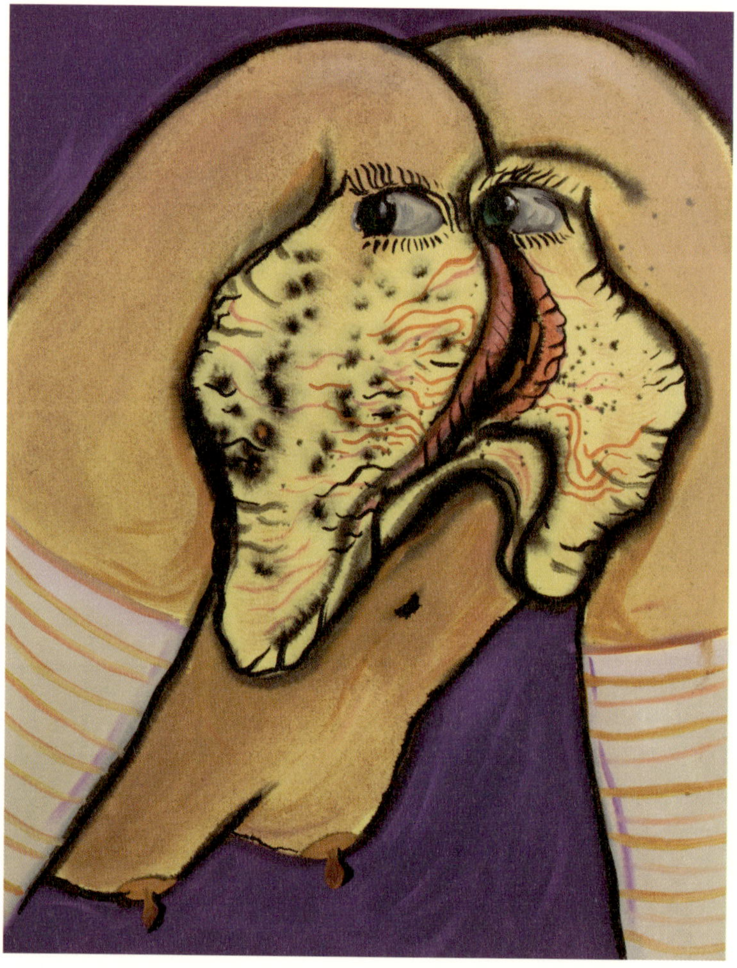

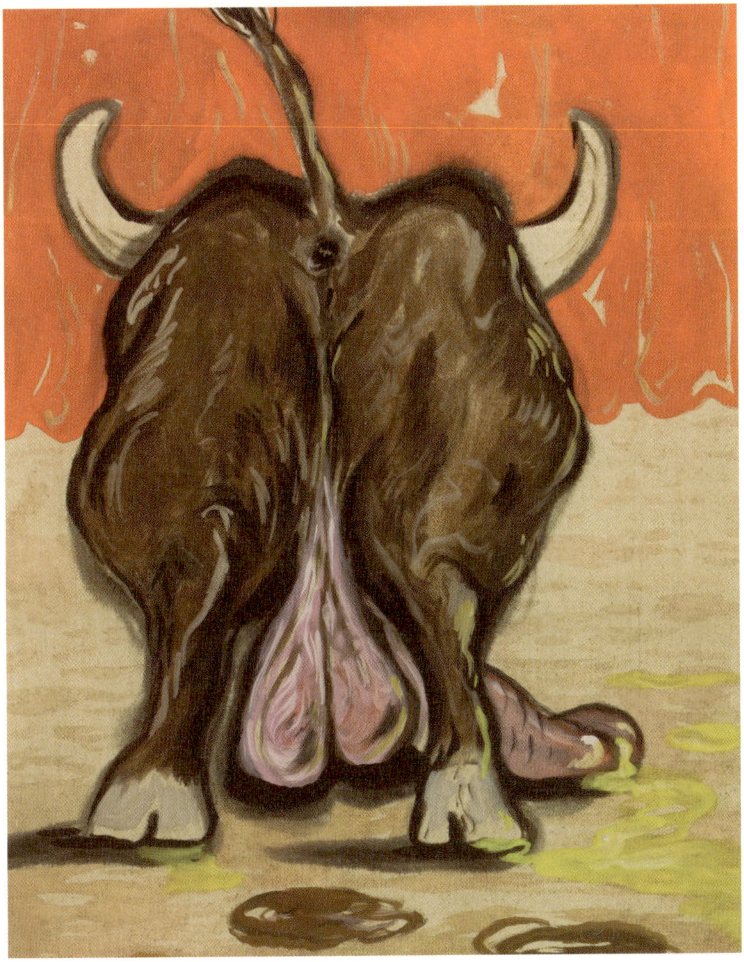

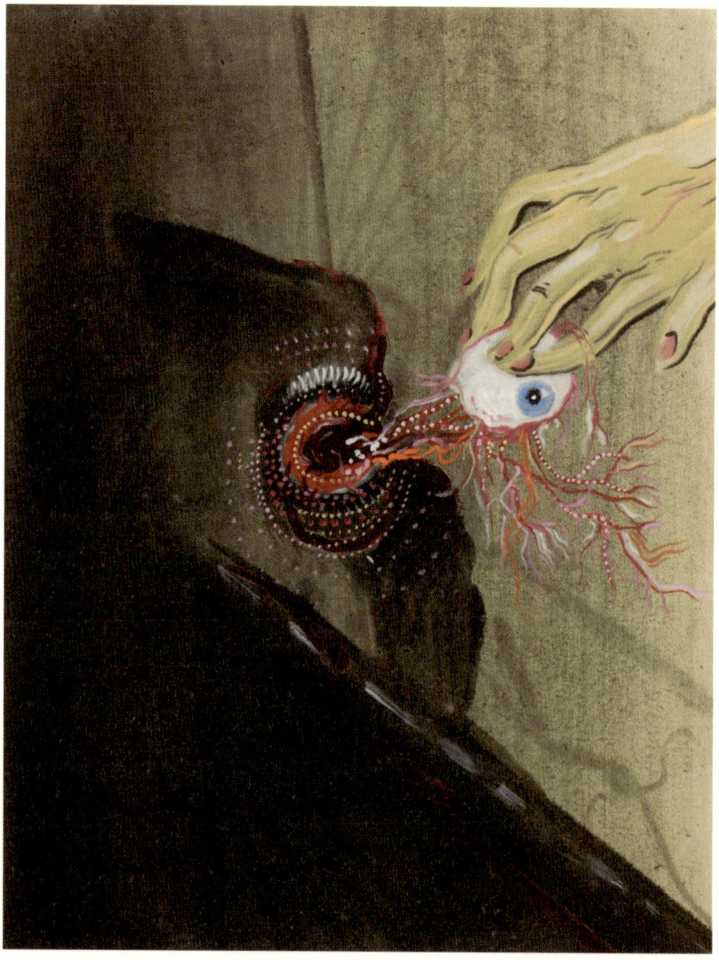

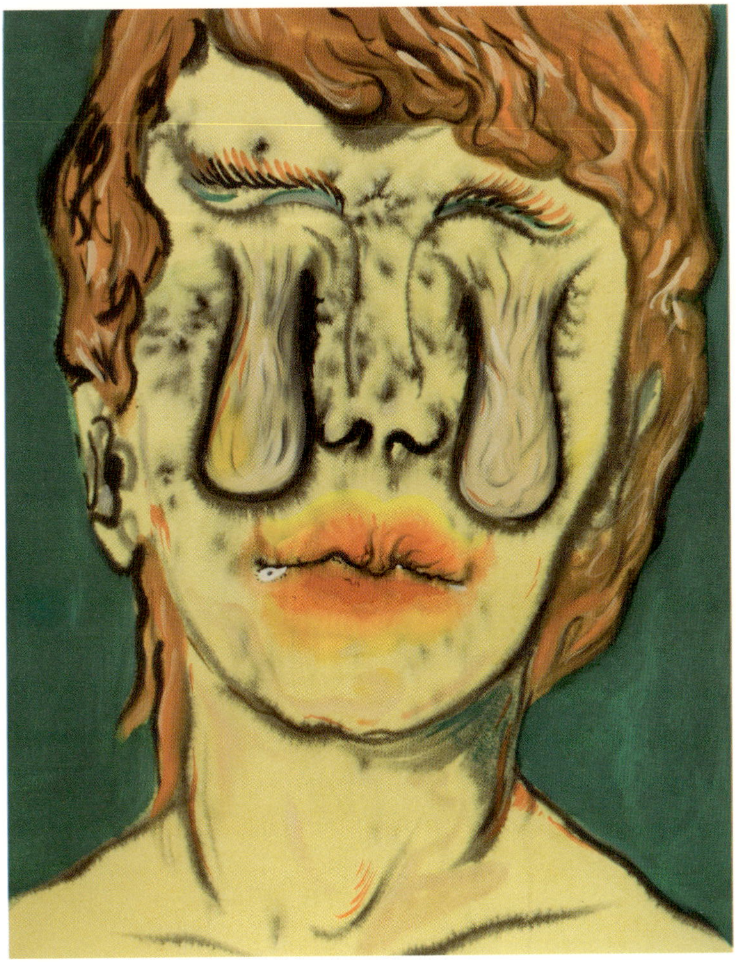

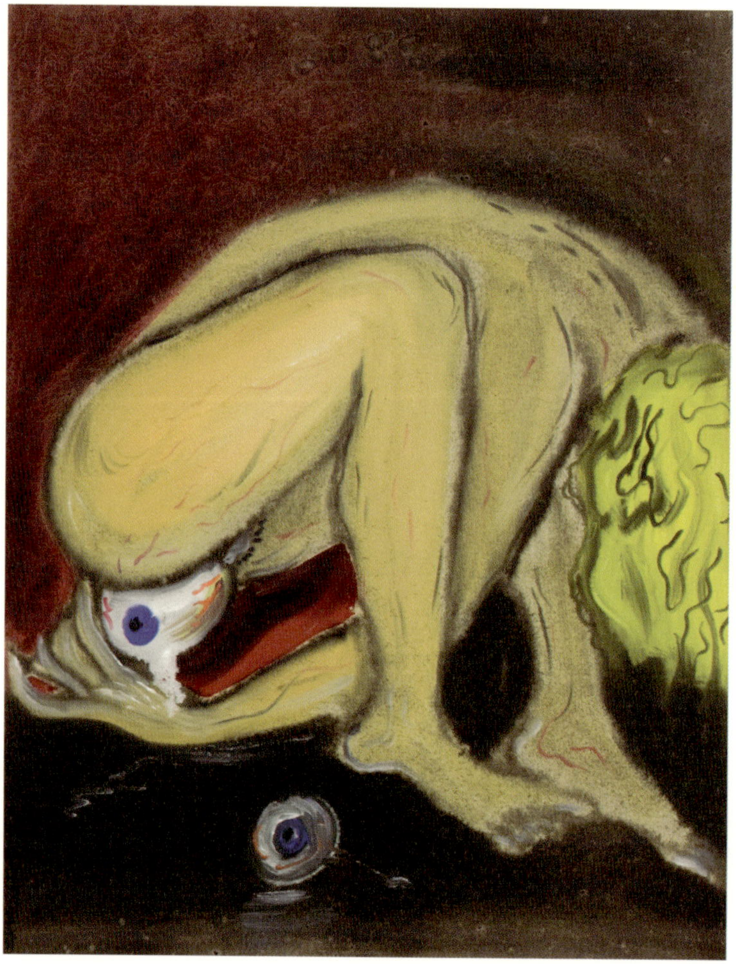

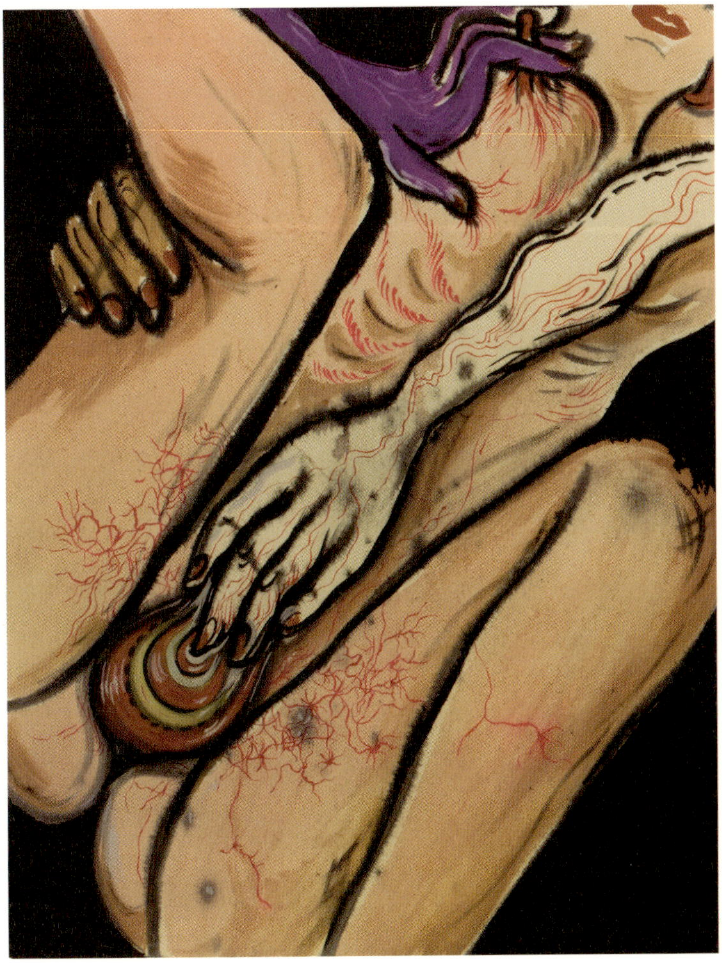

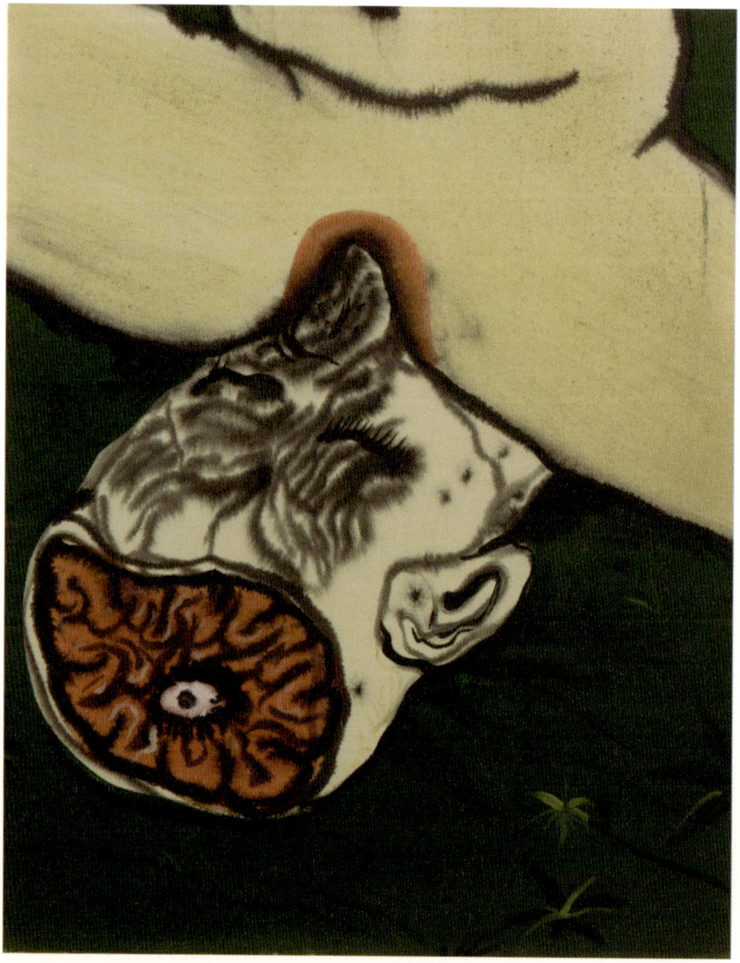

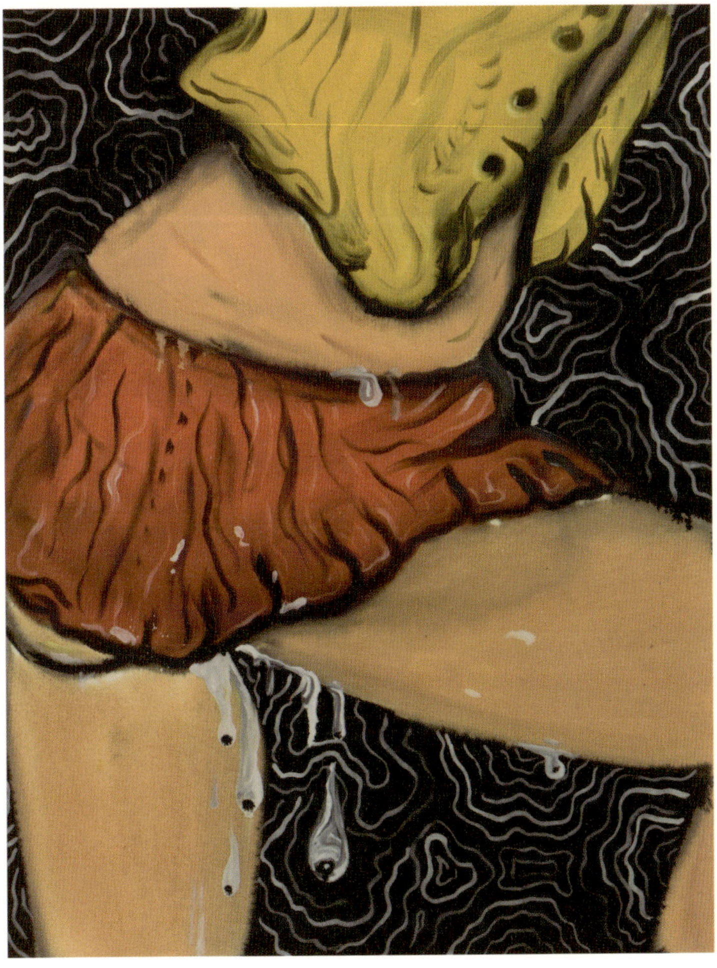

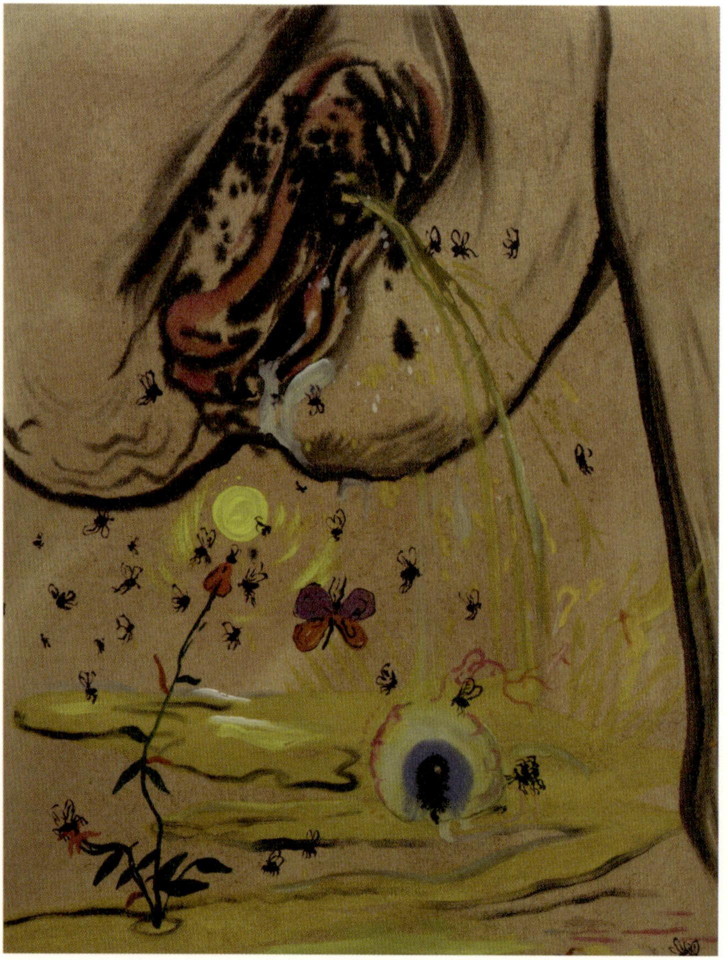

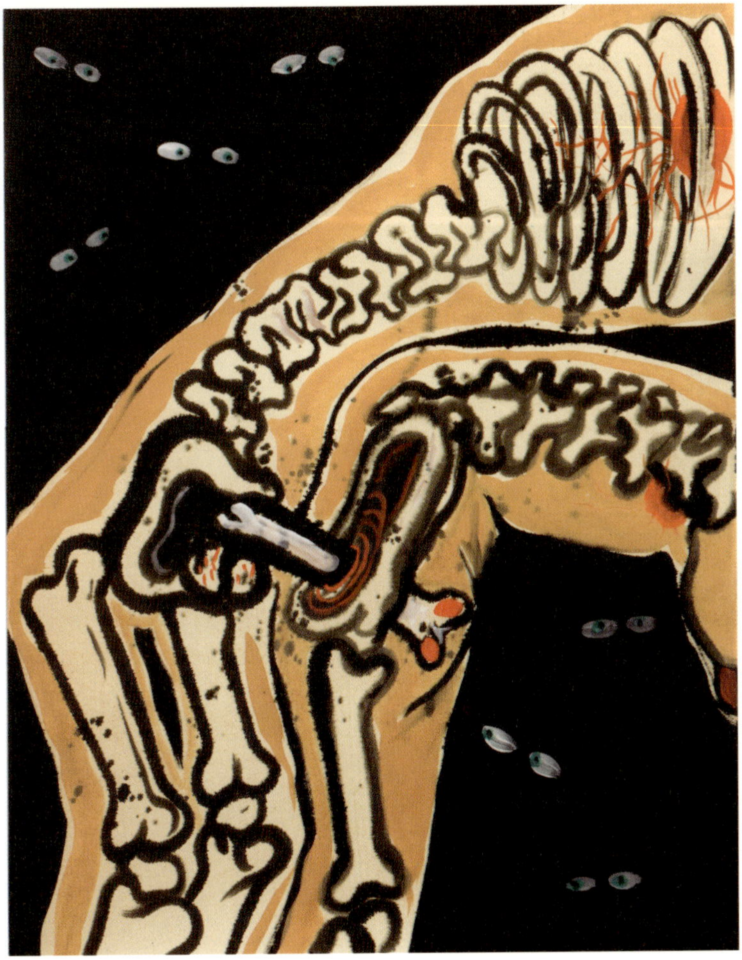

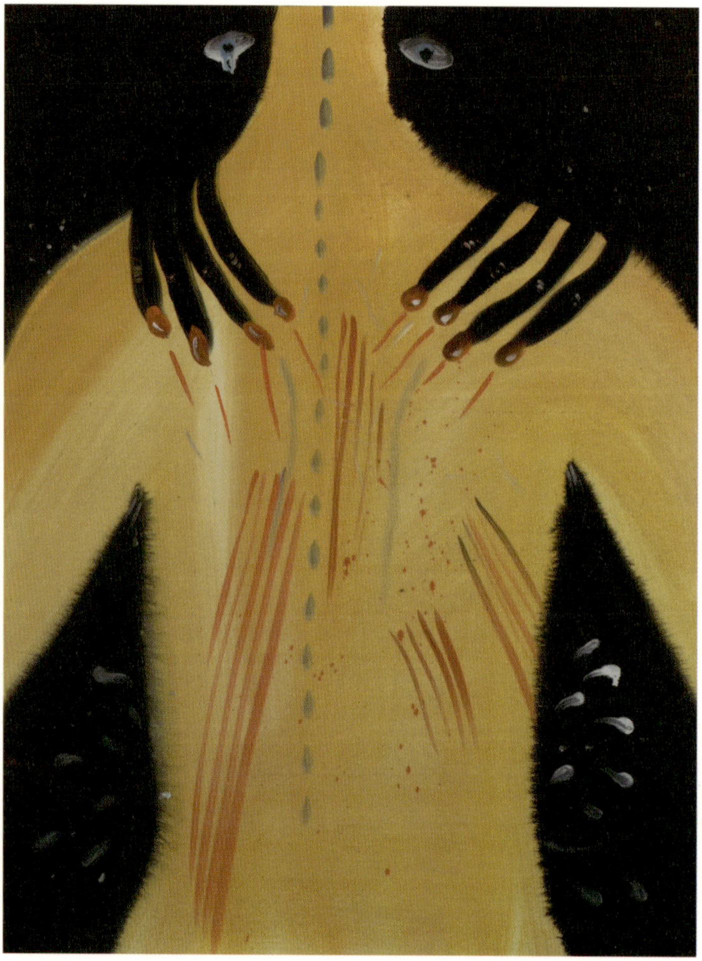

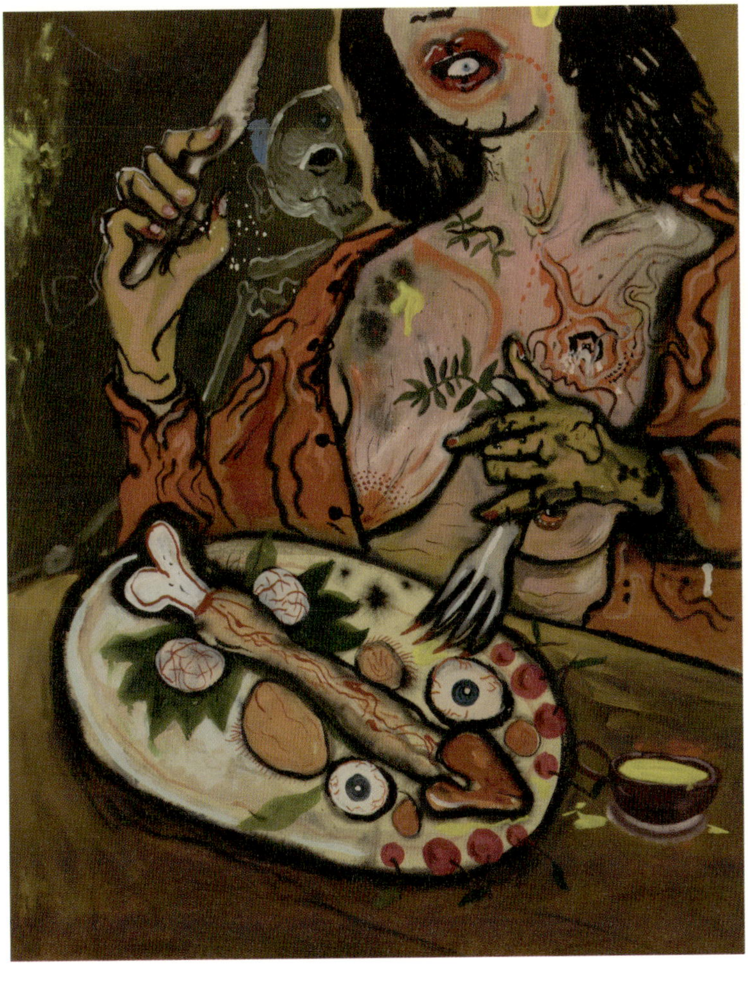

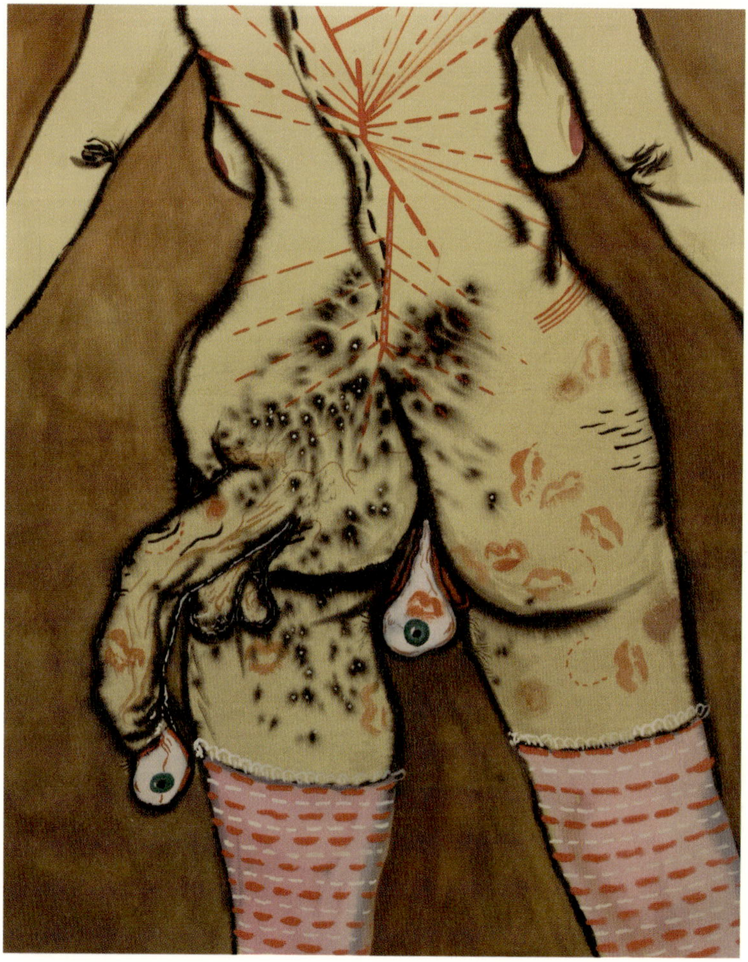

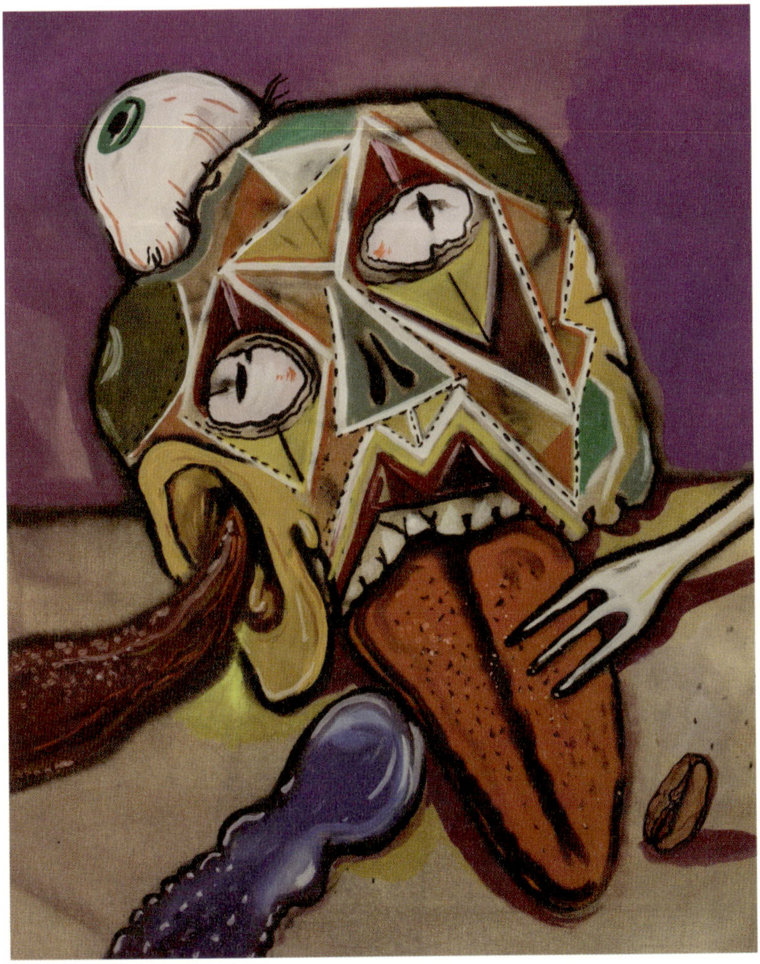

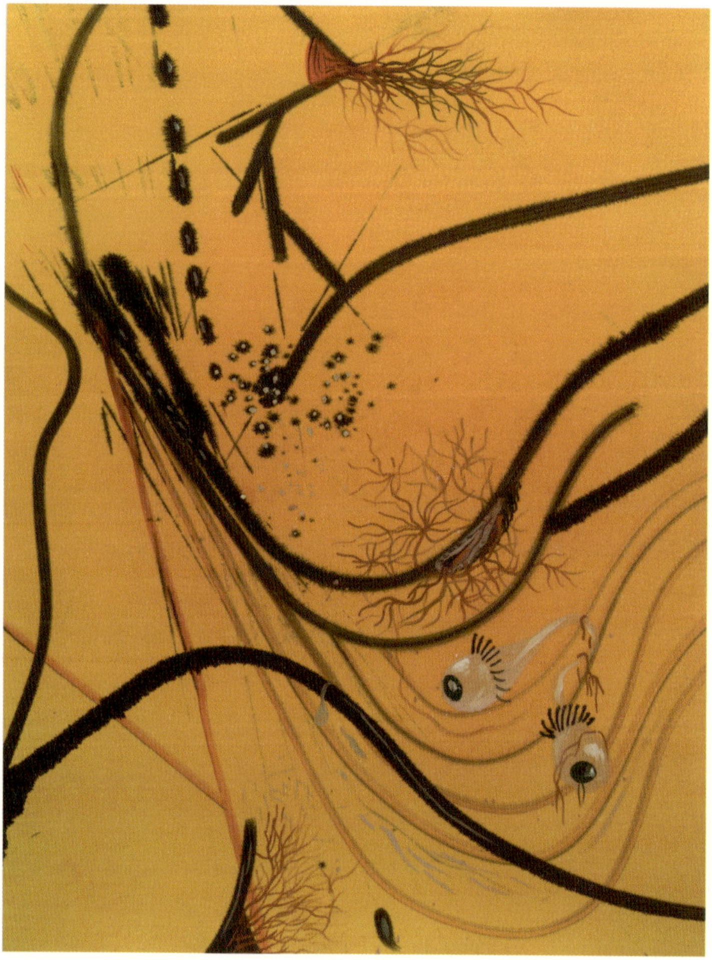

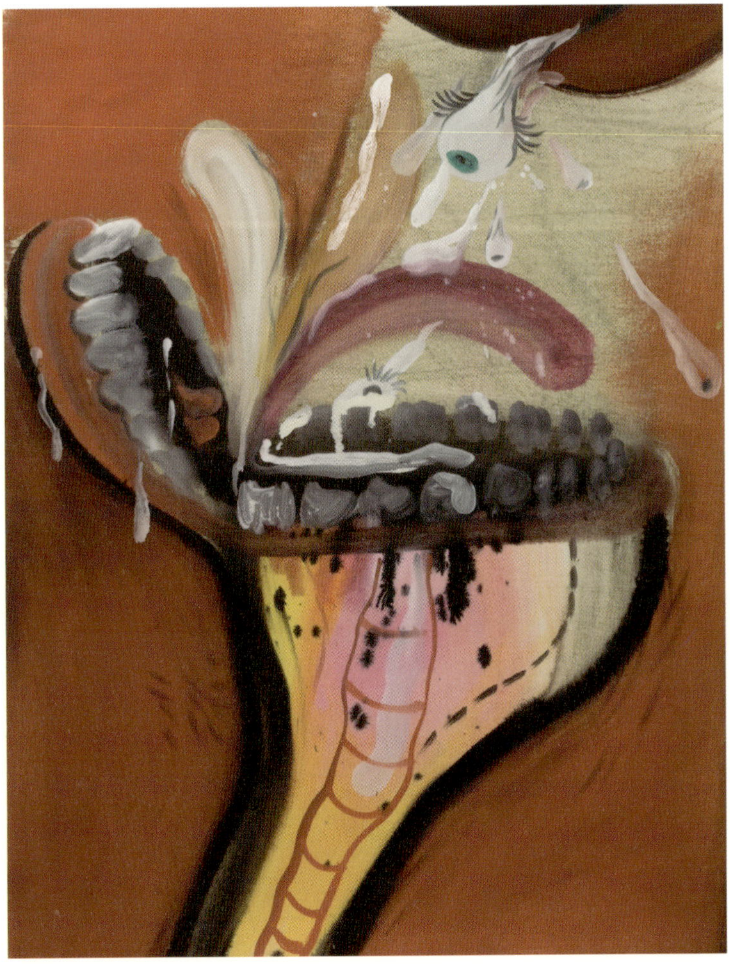

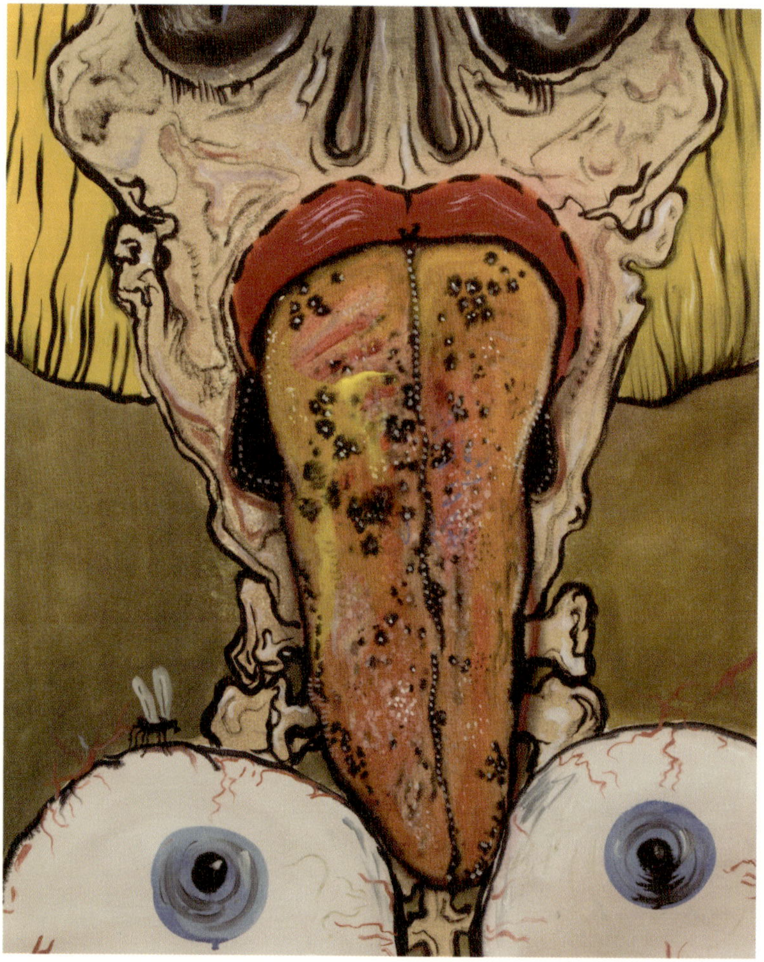

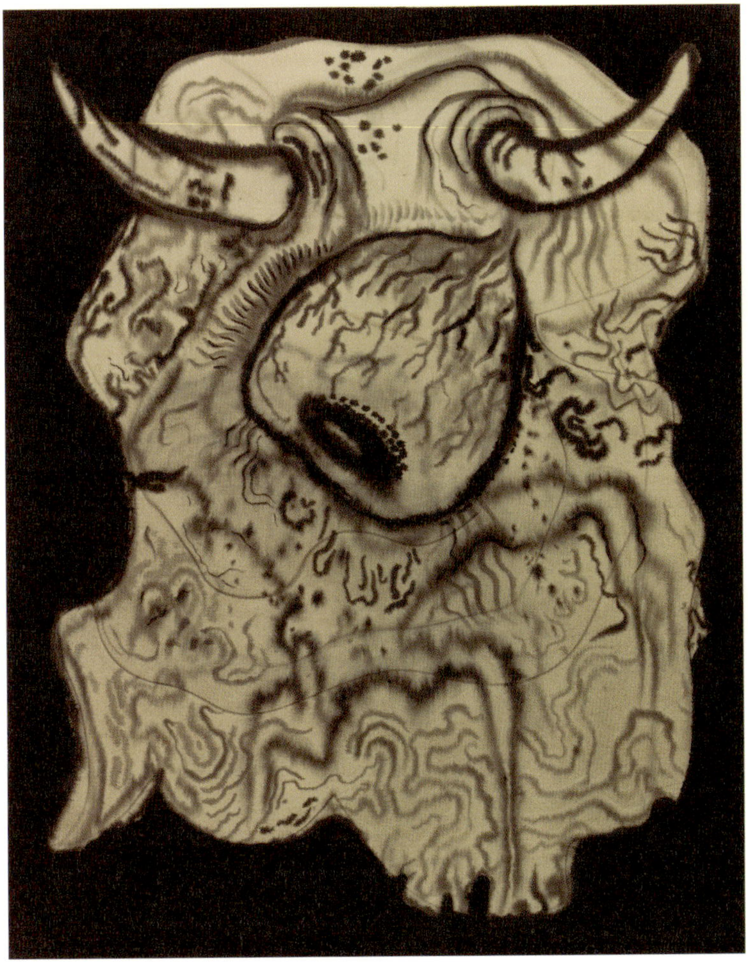

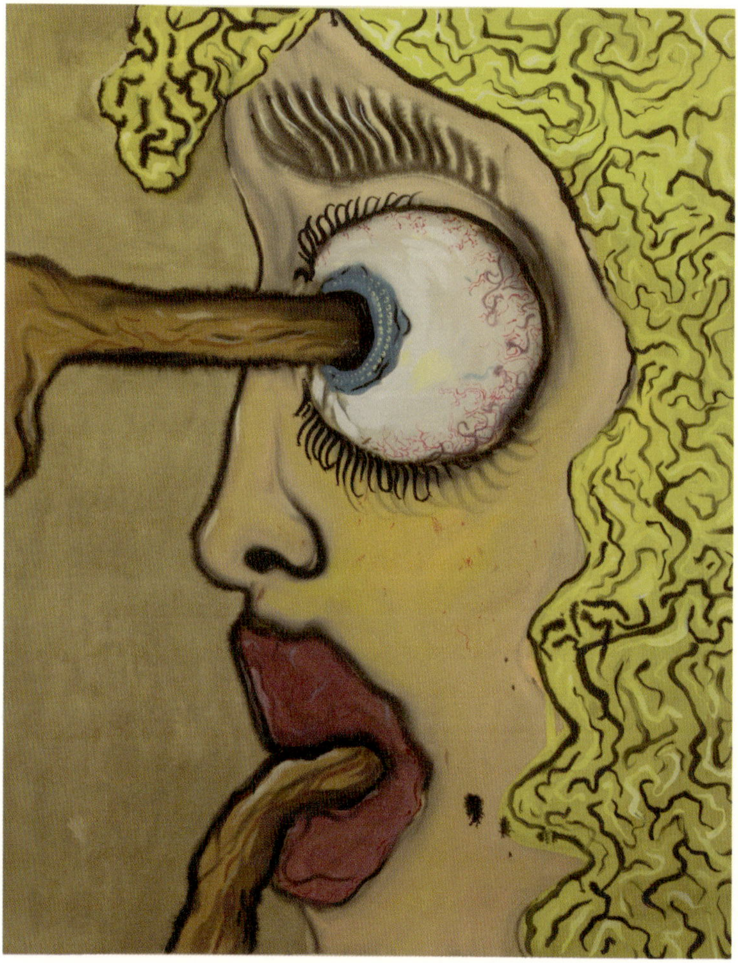

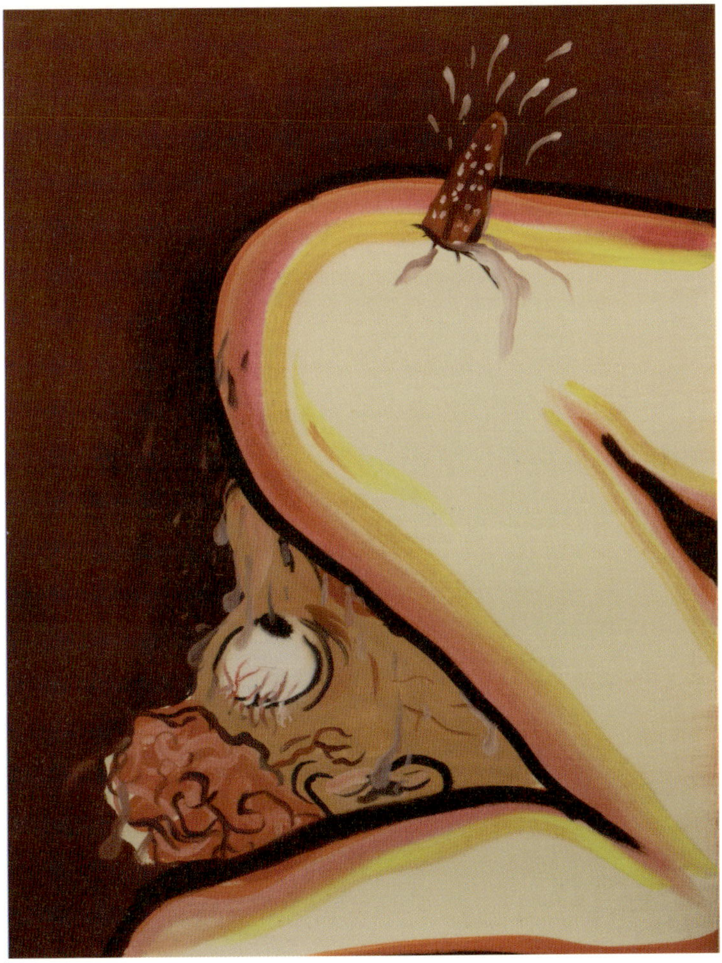

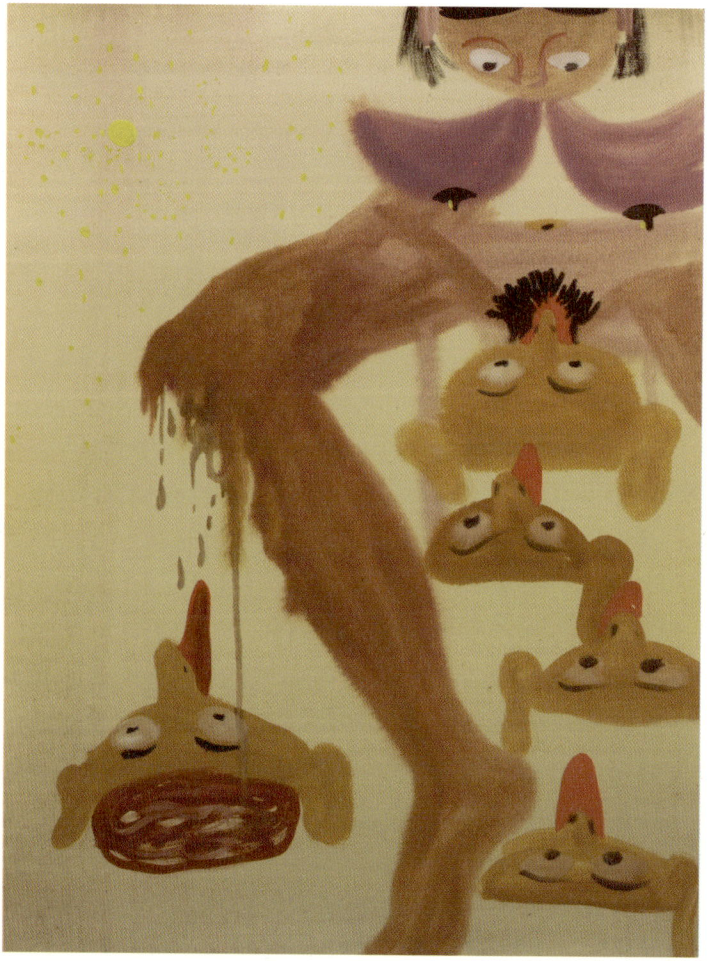

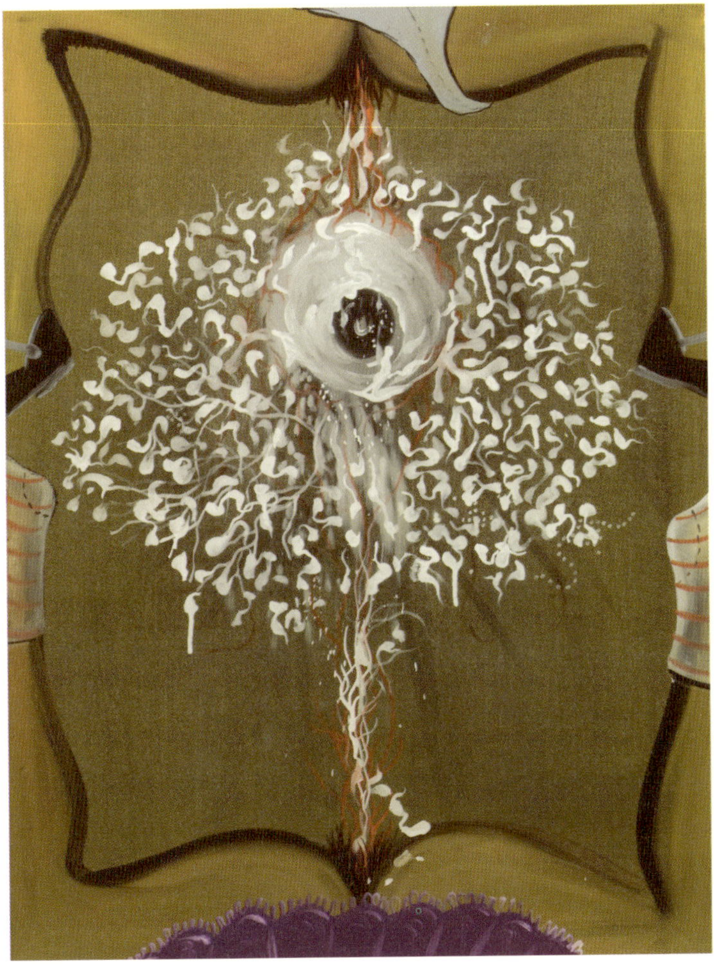

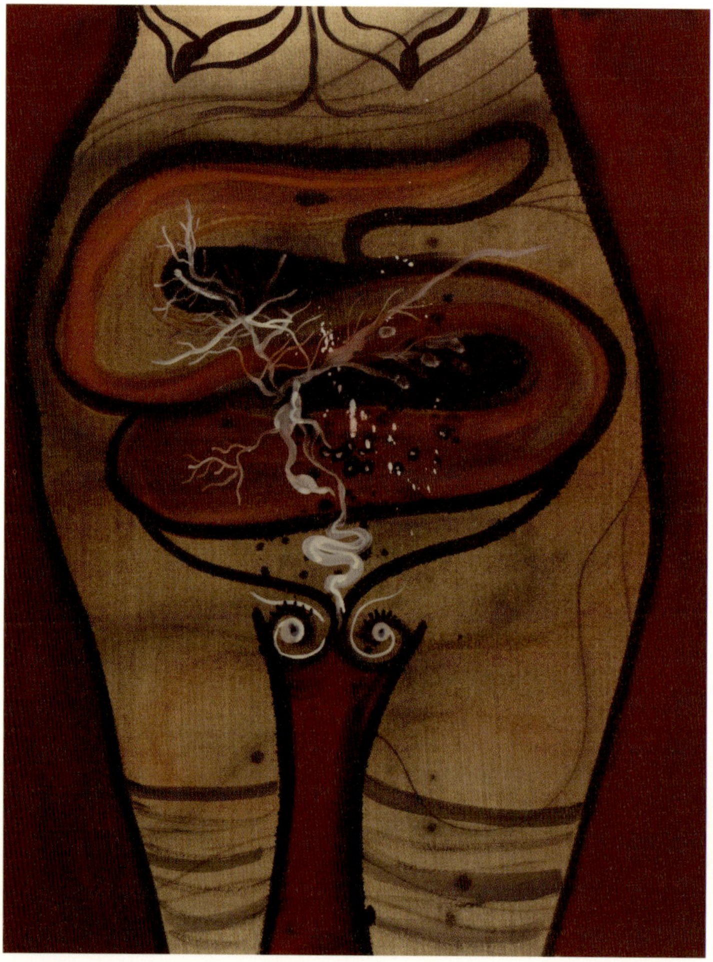

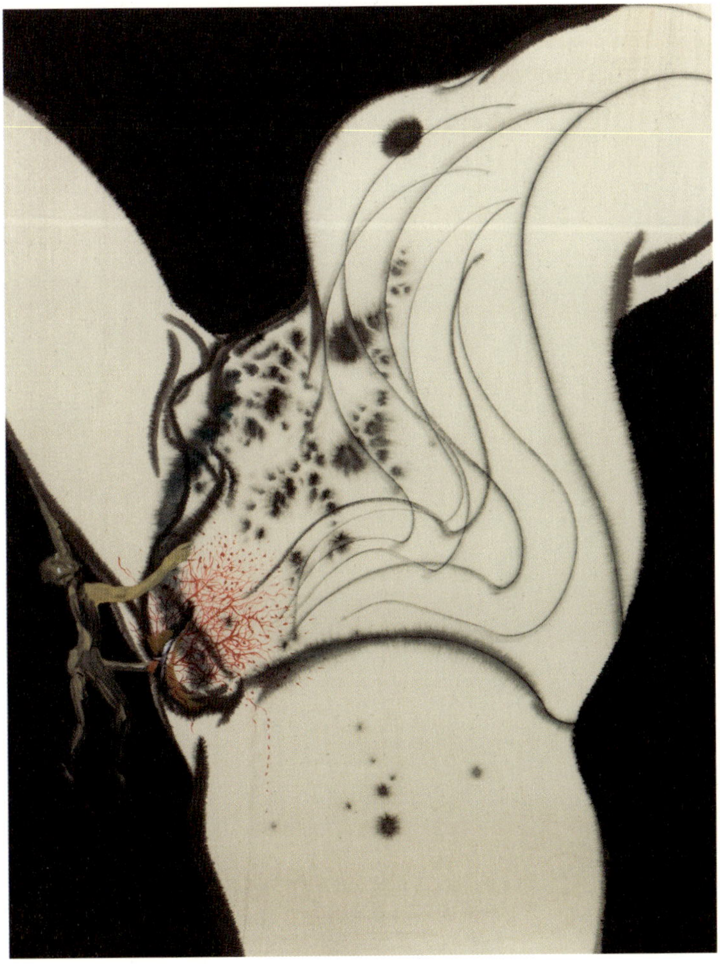

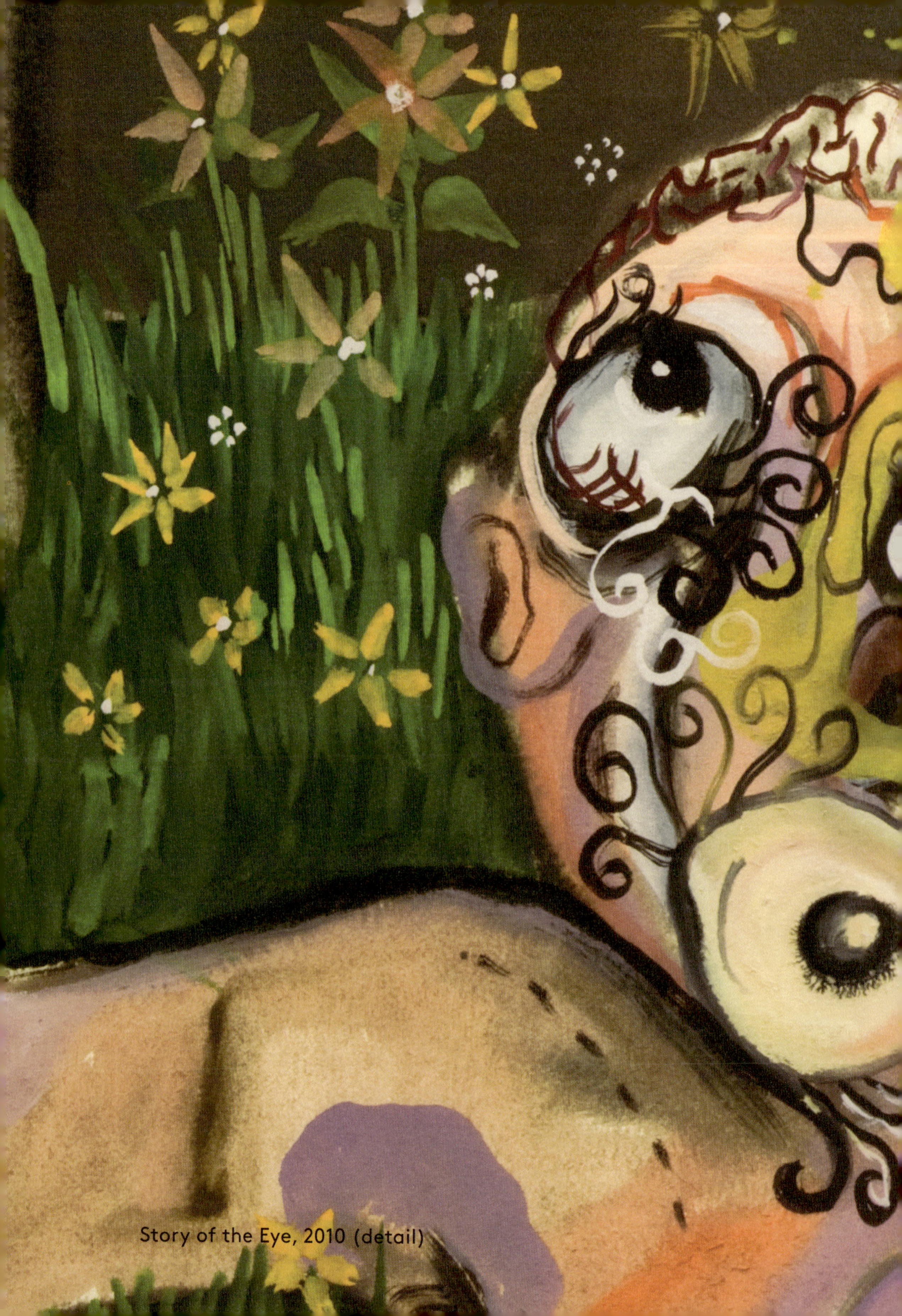

Story of the Eye, 2010 (detail)

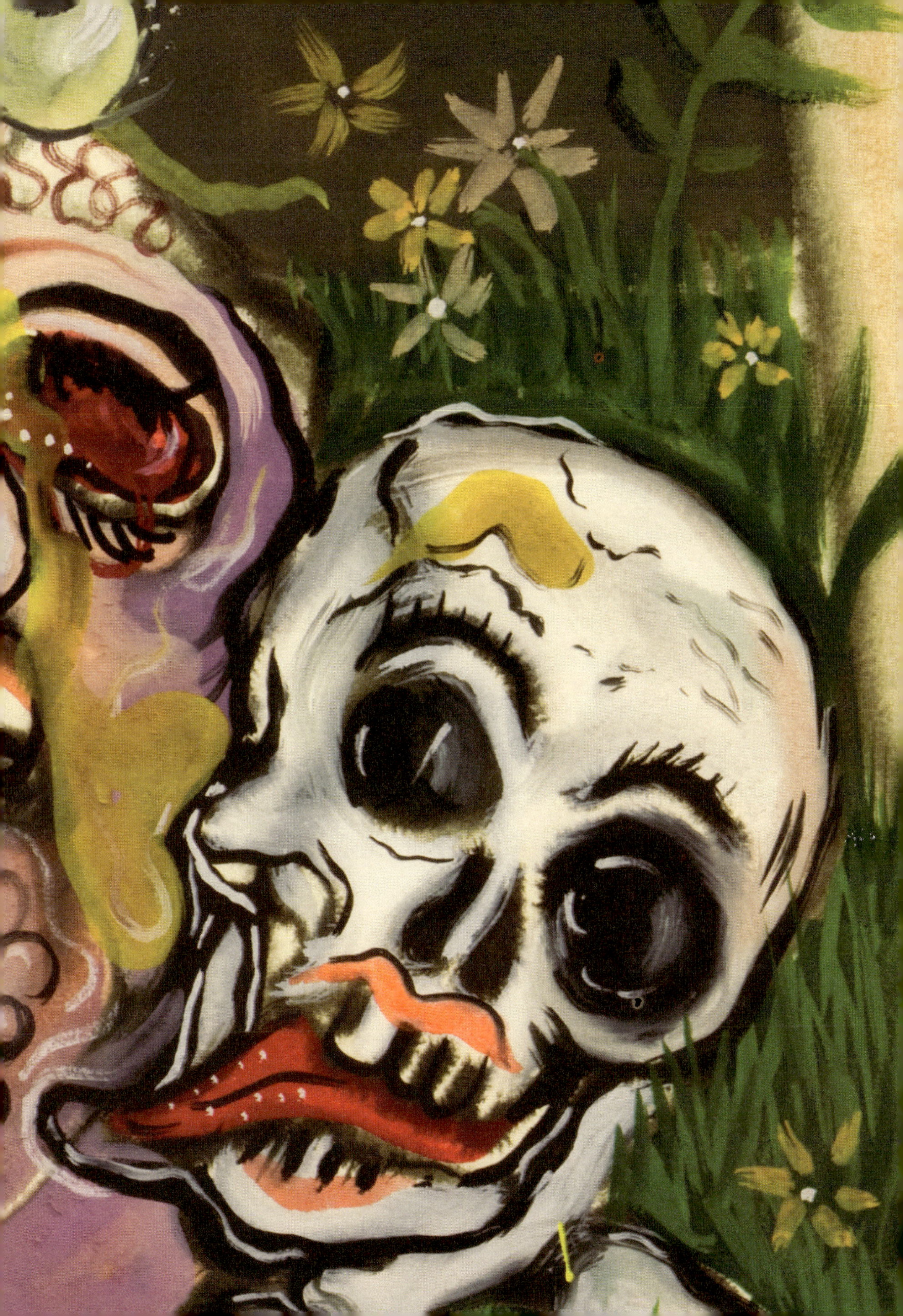

HISTORIA OKA

Jakub Julian Ziółkowski

I was troubled. Georges Bataille's *Story of the Eye* is certainly quite a challenge for a painter. Paintings and gouaches based on the notorious story were to be my presentation at the 8th Gwangju Biennale in Korea. Massimiliano Gioni, the curator, selected me for this task in the manner of someone looking for a guy to do a dirty job. Not everyone is able to kill, and even fewer people are capable of bringing their boss the victim's cut-off head with a bunch of juicy grapes placed inside a bloody, empty eyehole—plus a rose behind his ear. Although at the sight of flowing blood I pale and freeze, I became a dirty-job man.

At first, the curator was patient. Then he got very impatient because I was still struggling to find the right approach to Bataille's text. I read through the text looking for my own path. An old rule of thumb: before you jump into the water, learn how to swim and breathe slowly. I read the story my own way. The first time—a quick reconnaissance. The second time—looking at the language and the structure of the text, looking closely at the descriptions, the colors, the scenes. The third time—remembering the most powerful scenes, looking at motifs and symbols, searching for recesses, sweet seeds inside bitter fruit. The "eye" became a breath, an egg, a testicle, earth, sun, moon, cosmos, an atom, an embryo, a fetus, a slot, a gate, an entrance to the vagina, a hole gaping from the ground, a hole in the lavatory, a drop of semen, a reflection of light in the drop of semen, lips, a slimy ball of mozzarella cheese, a spherical teardrop, a drop of urine, dog poo in the street, a head, a third eye, a cylindrical ray of spiritual energy, an anus, a stained glass oval window in a church, the host, Christ's semen, a flickering lightbulb in the staircase of a black gallery, a phial filled with medicine, a suppository, a pill, an ice cube, candlelight, a fading spark, a rotund casket, a clod of earth, the larva of a worm, nothing, the number zero, the letter O. In many of the languages of Eastern Europe, including Polish, the word *eye* is *oko*. The word itself looks like a pair of eyes: O *k* O. Even the letter O is a metaphor for a kind of fishy, senile eye.

I was troubled. I think mounting that hill took me three months. And reaching the top took two or three weeks of tiresome marching for ten hours a day. The exhibition curator became increasingly impatient, and I felt a slight pressure on my back, which is both the worst and the best way to begin to get something done.

One day I prepared a pile of papers, as I usually do. I relaxed my eyes and hands. I got to work, I pinned the first sheet and painted a penis with a drop of semen. Then the next one, then the fourth, the eighth. I was squeezing my own juice from the story. A stream of gouaches burst forth. I submitted to the stream, to automatism. After this initial burst, I began each day with coffee and quick work. Every day, the same thing over and over again. There was only me and the eye and the stream pouring out of control. Quite soon my imagination ran wild. I created my own *Story of the Eye*, endlessly inventing new perversions and my own arrangements of vaginas and penises, experimenting with the composition of mucus, excrement, semen, slime, pain, and pleasure. My process became a kind of psychoanalysis. A Pandora's box had opened which I had never before experienced on this scale or in this form. As you can guess, the dirty-job man gets hired because he is destined to be the dirty-job man. This is his karma.

My karma consisted of fantasizing and draining my mind of hidden desires. I dreamt perverse dreams. The pile of painted papers grew rapidly. Then I paused, wondering where it was taking me. And then I knew: I was going to the source.

Returning to the text, I decided to integrate my personal story with Bataille's. Up until this moment it had been an interpretation, an emotional imprint in my mind; my reimagining of Bataille's story. Speeding, liberated, in the middle of the process, I suddenly started drawing the story's motifs. Sensitive to every scene, I traveled through the text marking the points that must be included in my story. When I completed 69 works, I decided it was a symbolic number and that I should end there. All the works are vertical, gouaches in erection, hung close to one another in a black space cut off from reality. Bataille's mind, my mind, one room, two stories in a black cage, more or less 5 x 5 meters, thick air, a windowless room. That is what it was supposed to look like.

Then I was troubled again. Everything was ready, the story was finished. But I was still working, still creating. Nothing else in life interested me; this work was my whole life. Whatever I did, whatever I painted, it all automatically referred to *Story of the Eye*. It took me a very long time to release myself from the burden of Bataille's story. In fact, I still have an obsession with the metaphor of the eye. Or perhaps this obsession has always been inside me. This is my business. Parts of this experience will always be with me. My language has been enriched and expanded, a Pandora's box has opened, fears have been peeled back; I'm one step ahead. This is my business.

The last time I was troubled by this project was when my father visited me. I tested my *Story of the Eye* on him. After all, it was he who had asked whether he could see the pile of papers lying on the floor. "Please yourself," I said. I made a short introduction about Bataille's story and the installation at the Biennale. Together we looked through the material, sheet after sheet, slowly. I looked at his face, deep in concentration. There was no anxiety there, no grimace, nothing, nothing at all. Only a bit of curiosity. At the end of the day, he is my father. He especially has the right to judge my work. He and my brother are men who enter the same room every day to operate on ureters and people with prostate cancer and phimosis. They give hope to the impotent, stitch together broken and torn penises, and take out strange objects that were put there by lovers and fighters of eternal forces.

He said, "It's OK, it's good, show me this book." He sat drinking coffee as he scanned Bataille's story. "Good, it's good," he kept saying. This is how my father got to know *Story of the Eye*.

I flew to Korea two or three days before the beginning of the Biennale. I was right on time: some of my works were hanging upside down. And there was a sign near the entrance to the installation saying that the piece was for adults only. That warning was part of the installation's "technical requirements." Well, let it be. Karma. Local young girls who worked at the Biennale were very excited and wanted to take pictures with me. For memory's sake, of course. I had never experienced anything like that before. I still don't understand it. I don't know what it was about. Maybe it was nothing at all. I don't have a remarkable appearance, nothing special, I am normal, nobody recognizes me on the street, so maybe it was all about this body of work? Maybe they were fantasizing about a romp with some guy or another, as long as he was relatively young and appeared to have a perverse attitude? Bataille directs people to the very source of their perversions. Maybe he helped me to unmask the hidden erotic desires of this audience. Perhaps.

Or do people see only what they want to see? Perhaps the exception to this rule is the fortunate group of people who have successfully reached the conclusion of their psychoanalysis.

I saw *Story of the Eye* installed for a second time at an exhibition of Dakis Joannou's collection at the DESTE Foundation for Contemporary Art in Athens. I did not experience any new emotions. After all, time had passed. When you're constantly doing something, working on new paintings, the earlier works quickly become old. They seem like a faded state of mind. This is how I see it. I am not very attached to what has happened in the past, although I don't necessarily see forward movement as a mark of something better. Perhaps I am still too young for such artistic sentiments. Whatever the case, I did not feel ashamed of this work. It is a very peculiar and homogenous work, powerfully armored. It should keep its power, and I hope it will.

Some time ago there was a new edition of *Story of the Eye* published in Polish. I think this is a very good sign. Earlier editions were very difficult to find; they were hidden but not forgotten. Perhaps they were desired even more intensely.

LIST OF WORKS

Untitled, 2008
Oil on canvas
80 × 70 cm

Untitled (Bobby), 2008
Oil on canvas
120 × 110 cm

Untitled, 2009
Oil on canvas
40 × 32 cm

Untitled, 2009
Oil on canvas
120 × 110 cm

Untitled, 2009
Oil on canvas
210 × 170 cm

Monk, 2009
Oil on canvas
38 × 48 cm

Untitled, 2010
Oil on canvas
38 × 48 cm

Untitled (King of Israel), 2010
Oil on canvas
190 × 165 cm

Story of the Eye, 2010
Gouache on paper
69 drawings, dimensions variable

Skin and Bread, 2011
Oil on canvas
190 × 240 cm

The Blood (The Holy Blood), 2011
Oil on panel
76 × 61 cm

Untitled / Woman in a Cap, 2011
Oil on canvas
55 × 46 cm

Dark Self Portrait, 2011
Oil on canvas
90 × 70 cm

ARTIST BIO

Jakub Julian Ziółkowski was born in 1980 in the small Polish town of Zamość. Ziółkowski's paintings and drawings of organs without bodies and bodies without organs question the very epistemological foundation of our senses. With a style that blends grotesque realism with heavenly surrealism, Ziółkowski discovers the microcosmic in the galactic, confounding our ordinary understanding of the body and its limitations.

Ziółkowski has had solo exhibitions at a number of international institutions, including *Raw Thoughts* at Hauser & Wirth, Zurich, Switzerland (2013); *Hydra 2012* at the Hydra Workshop, Greece; *Skin and Bread* at the Foksal Gallery Foundation, Warsaw, Poland (2012); *In Utero* at Parasol Unit, London, England (2011); *History of the Eye* at the DESTE Foundation for Contemporary Art, Athens, Greece (2011); *Hokaina* at the Zachęta National Gallery of Art, Warsaw, Poland (2010), and at the Centre d'Art Contemporain, Geneva, Switzerland (2009). He has also been included in group exhibitions, including the 55th Venice Biennale (2013); the 8th Gwangju Biennale, Korea (2010); and *The Generational: Younger Than Jesus* at the New Museum for Contemporary Art, New York (2009), which brought Ziółkowski to international attention. Jakub Julian Ziółkowski lives and works in Zamość and Krakow.

AUTHOR BIO

Cecilia Alemani is the Donald R. Mullen, Jr. Curator and Director of High Line Art, the public art program presented by Friends of the High Line. Since her appointment in 2011, she has commissioned and curated a number of projects by, among others, El Anatsui, Uri Aran, John Baldessari, Carol Bove, Simone Forti, Gilbert & George, Raymond Pettibon, Mungo Thomson, Virginia Overton, and Andra Ursuta. Alemani is also the curator of Frieze Projects in New York, where she has organized new commissions, including works by Latifa Echakhch, Liz Glynn, Joel Kyack, and Marianne Vitale, as well as historical tributes to artists such as John Ahearn and Gordon Matta-Clark.

In 2009, Alemani was curatorial director of X Initiative, a yearlong experimental project space, for which she curated No Soul For Sale: A Festival of Independents with Maurizio Cattelan and Massimiliano Gioni. The festival traveled to the Tate Modern in London in 2010. *Charley Independents*, edited by Alemani, Cattelan, Gioni, and Ali Subotnick, and published by the DESTE Foundation for Contemporary Art in 2010, documented the artists' collectives and nonprofit organizations that appeared at No Soul For Sale.

I would like to thank Jakub Julian Ziółkowski, whose magic touch has turned the world upside down and inside out, leaving us disoriented and wondering. I am grateful to Cecilia Alemani, whose fascination with Ziółkowski's visceral take on the world has deepened since her first visit to his studio in Krakow. My heartfelt appreciation to Massimiliano Gioni who has commissioned all of the essays, to Karen Marta for her unwavering enthusiasm, and to Brendan Dugan, for his thoughtful design of this book.

—Dakis Joannou

Jakub Julian Ziółkowski
2000 Words

Commissioning Editor: Massimiliano Gioni
Editor: Karen Marta
Design: An Art Service
Editorial Assistant: Quinn Lewington
Coordinators: Regina Alivisatos and Dustin Cosentino
Registrar: Natasha Polymeropoulos
Copy Editors: Miles Champion and Grace Moss
Production: The Production Department

Published by:
The DESTE Foundation for Contemporary Art
Filellinon 11 & Em. Pappa St.
N. Ionia 142 34, Athens
www.deste.gr

Cover: Jakub Julian Ziółkowski, detail from *Story of the Eye*, 2010
Thank you to Joanna Diem and Aleksandra Urbanska at Foksal Gallery Foundation, Warsaw, and Makiko Ushiba

Distributed in the Americas by:
ARTBOOK | D.A.P.
155 Sixth Avenue, 2nd Floor
New York, NY 10013
www.artbook.com

Distributed in Europe by:
Buchhandlung Walther König
Ehrenstrasse 4
50672 Köln
www.buchhandlung-walther-koenig.de

Printed in Greece by Alta Grafico S.A. Printing and Graphic Arts

ISBN: 978-618-5039-05-9

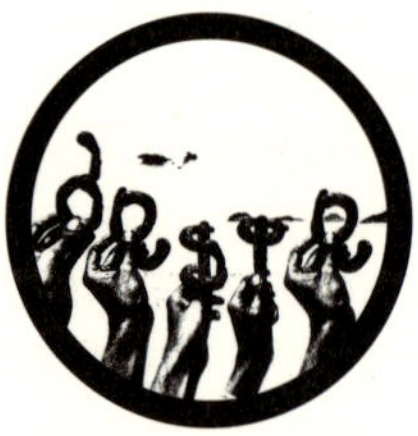